ENDORSEMENTS

INSPIRITIONAL Milli's experience as a mother who traveled the journey with her son was heart-wrenching and uplifting. The book was a page-turner and a must read for every mother. The author has shown me how much impact we all have in helping a patient and their family find the road to recovery. Bonnie Sidoff, Providence Emergency Room Physician

PULLED INTO THE STRUGGLE The writing style "pulled" me along to the celebratory ending. Here is drama: real life drama. Here is transparency: the author aptly records each person's struggle including accident victim Mark's. Here is triumph: A Time to Dance, a perfect title. Dr. Herbert E. Anderson, former pastor, Hinson Church.

UNIVERSAL APPEAL Milli's book - Timeless: speaking to all generations and cultures. Captivating: confronting issues of life and death. Inspiring: lifting the human spirit. We observe a champion, carrying the banner for all in demonstrating and proclaiming the triumph of faith, devotion, and prayer over even the most cruel of life's adversities. Martha E. Baker, Educator, Chaplain, Speech Pathologist

EMBODIMENT OF FAITH AND ENDURANCE Trials are not meant to be easy for they are the seed bed of faith. Through trials people seek out the practical presence of God. Each page of this book clearly describes the honest human struggle with this process. In the end, extra faith and endurance prevail. Ron Willis, Pastor

CAPTIVATING As an educator who works with both mentally and physically handicapped people I was captivated by Mark's incredible story told from a mother's heart. This awesome book enhanced my faith and made me feel an unwavering strength and identity. I have never seen such a practical hands-on guide dealing with a severe trauma. This book makes a huge contribution to society. Laurie Trybom, Adult Basic Skills Instructor

PAIN, GOD'S MEGAPHONE The author's honest book typifies C. S. Lewis' famous axiom, "Pain is God's megaphone." Her life affirms that when we lean into pain rather than running from it, God lovingly teaches us depth about His character that we might miss in comfortable circumstances. "In ALL things God works for the good of those who love Him." Dr. Ruth Knutson, Navigator Staff

PRACTICAL TIPS TO COPE, COMFORT, AND CONFRONT With a succinct style, Laughlin journals her family's tragedy and creates a wealth of practical tips to cope with, to comfort through, and to confront the conundrum of being human in a suffering world. Linda Highman, Educator

READER BECOMES PARTICIPANT An amazing, honest, vulnerable rendering of the author's feelings that draws the reader into the tragedy as a participant. An easy read and yet it was not "easy" to read as you agonized with the family along their long, unpredictable journey. Dolores Preble, Women's Representative, The Navigators

A WORTHY READ I couldn't put this book down. The author demonstrates her vulnerability as a loving mother baring her soul in crisis. Her unabashed honesty brought me to tears as I shared in her sorrow and joy. This inspiring, worthy-read will assist and encourage readers who are going through any long, hard journey. Dolores Bixby, avid reader

REMARKABLE For caregivers and those doing through a crisis this book is a must. The Thought/Action Provokers pertinent to each chapter are invaluable. Kathleen Nielsen, Retired Executive Secretary

PROVOCATIVE A provocative read in which the author puts into words the deep emotion of a mother going through a crisis which both challenges and blesses the reader. Laughlin's account of this journey honors God and provides hope for anyone going through a tragedy. Dr. Dwayne Frank, Professor Emeritus

CANDID The author masterfully tells this crisis recovery story. A Time to Dance will be an encouragement for anyone going through difficult life altering experiences. Phyllis Sahlin, Retired Educator

A TIME TO DANCE

A TIME TO DANCE

✦

One Family's Recovery from Catastrophe

Milli Laughlin

iUniverse LLC
Bloomington

A TIME TO DANCE
One Family's Recovery from Catastrophe

iUniverse books may be ordered through booksellers or by contacting:

iUniverse LLC
1663 Liberty Drive
Bloomington, IN 47403
www.iuniverse.com
1-800-Authors (1-800-288-4677)

Because of the dynamic nature of the Internet, any Web addresses or links contained in this book may have changed since publication and may no longer be valid

Unless otherwise stated, Scripture taken from the HOLY BIBLE: NEW INTERNATIONAL VERSION ®. NIV®. Copyright © 1973, 1978, 1984 by International Bible Society. Used by permission of Zondervan.

The "NIV" and "New International Version" trademarks are registered in the United States Patent and Trademark Office by International Bible Society.

ISBN: 978-0-5953-6389-6 (sc)
ISBN: 978-0-5958-0826-7 (ebk)

Printed in the United States of America

iUniverse rev. date: 04/17/2012

TO

Mark, whose drive to achieve is relentless

TABLE OF CONTENTS

FOREWORD

Sometimes a Mother with three preschoolers hurries and says a quick prayer "Thank you, Father, for our food. In Jesus Name, Amen." But not so in the year 1983. For any one of my three girls would squeal out, "Mom, don't forget to pray for Mark." And so it was, for a year, our girls prayed for Mark five times a day: before meals, nap, and bedtime. And Mom couldn't ever just say, "And we pray for Mark." We had to pray specifically: for Mark to wake up, to open his eyes, to swallow, to sit up, to walk, and on and on.

What did we learn from Mark's experience? We learned from the prayers of our children that a childlike faith moves mountains and that God is in control whatever the outcome.

A Time to Dance is the story of a young graduate student who loved his family and God. However, he experienced a tragedy that affected everything: his studies, dating, family, faith, and sports.

Mark's story is an uphill journey of uncertainty, hope, sorrow, and faith. The writing was painful for his mom, Milli, but also helped her heal. The story is a work of love and faith and drawn from many sources: family, friends, pastors, hospital personnel, sermons and journals. Milli does not write with rose-colored glasses. She shows the gamut of human emotions in real life: love, compassion, happiness, heartbreak, anger, success and failure. We see a glimpse into the heart and soul of a family who together and alone faces the challenge of their lifetime.

As this book is published, my prayers are simply these: —That the experiences of Mark's family–the triumphs and failures, the questions they have wrestled with and some answers they have learned–may encourage others to grow in their faith and commitment to God.

—That any reader who does not know for certain where they would go if they died tonight, would settle that forever.

—That anyone who may be going through a crisis now or is on the journey of recovery may find the Thought/Action Provokers at the end of the book to help them answer their questions or to find activities that will aid in their recovery.

—That as a nurse practitioner, all we in the medical profession would evaluate our words and actions when giving care to families; that we would guard our tongues and become a Shirley or Carol in this story. I pray we will also remember that God is truly the great Physician.

—That a doubting, cynical world will be drawn to the many examples in this story of Christian friends living out their faith, caring, and sacrificing one for another, and will see that this does make a difference in life.

Obviously these prayers go beyond what this book can accomplish, but these are still my prayers.

My three young girls learned that healing is slow, and that God's timing is not our timing. I heard more than once, "Mom, is God listening? Well, why doesn't He hurry up and make Mark…" However, they never tired of praying and never gave up on God. I still pray, "Oh, God, make the memories of <u>A Time to Dance</u> live on in our hearts forever."

Mary Ann Zimmerman, R.N., P.N.P.
Prayer partner and friend

ACKNOWLEDGEMENTS

In the process of refining my book, Ruth Knutson came along side, mentored, and encouraged me. Her belief that this book has a valuable message for readers who want to help others through crises mirrored the convictions of my writer friends. They all generously took time from their own writings, tasks, and engagements to reassure, and affirm me.

To you, Ruth, and that coterie of supportive writers who echoed your belief, "this book has a vital message,"

thank you.

I extend heartfelt thanks to Drs. Michael J. Markham, Dr. Gary A. Ward, and the medical personnel too numerous to mention by name, who provided excellent care for Mark; and to our extended family and friends who helped us survive our family crisis. A special thanks to Dr. Herb Anderson, Mark's fellow biker, who watched and waited for weeks in the same Portland hospital for his four-year old son to regain consciousness but then emerge severely handicapped, and years later have a similar experience with his wife, Betsy. How obvious it was that he, and other friends, who had suffered severe losses, felt our pain.

INTRODUCTION

Even though head injury occurs in the United State every 16 seconds, we felt isolated and alone. Although we were helpless and all seemed hopeless, God heard our continual cries and sustained us step by step, day by day.

No one is exempt. Individuals suffer a myriad of losses. All readers have probably experienced a crisis or are presently going through one (it is estimated that a person experiences six crises in a lifetime).

Denial, anger, bargaining, depression and acceptance are common in crises (Grief Counseling and Grief Therapy, pp. 11-17, J. William Worden, Springer Publishing Company, Inc., 1982). Our nightmare, coping with a son with a catastrophic insult, was no exception.

There was little information, except in medical literature, that helped guide us through the maze in our bewildering journey. If only there had been a personal story that honestly and openly spoke of the extreme ups and downs that families might experience.

We gradually learned that the bizarre and overwhelming process was a normal part of grieving. This fact helped us slowly progress to a "new normal" after a long, laborious, unpredictable recovery pattern.

In the appendix, "When Going Through a Crisis," the author points out practical steps toward physically, emotionally and spiritually healing. The Thought/ Action Provoker questions relevant to each chapter help readers to further reflect on the subject and to relate our family's crisis to hardships in their own lives.

Milli Laughlin

1

MEDICAL EMERGENCY 911

o o o o o o o o o o o o o o o o o o o o o o o o o o o o o o o o

The Almighty has his own purposes.

—Abraham Lincoln

Half awake in the middle of the night, I was startled by a noise I could not identify. Were animals fighting? No. The horrible sound was coming from Mark's bedroom in our daylight basement.

As I leaped out of bed my husband, Bob, awoke.

"What's wrong? What's wrong?"

"I don't know, but the noise is coming from Mark's room."

We flew downstairs.

On the bed lay our 23 year-old son, his arms interlocked, his body stiff. With clenched teeth he convulsed, frothing at the mouth.

"Mark!" I screamed. Bob was right behind me and cried out, too.

Whirling around, I bolted upstairs, grabbed our cordless phone and rushed back downstairs. Shakily I dialed 911, Medical Emergency. In a quaking voice, I described Mark's condition and gave the dispatcher our address.

"Turn him onto his side immediately," the dispatcher ordered. "That way he won't choke to death."

In spite of Mark's dead weight and rigidity, Bob, with presence of mind, forced him onto his left side. Using his knees, Bob braced our son in that position.

Even while the dispatcher was giving me information, blood gushed from Mark's mouth, running down into his tousled, blond hair. Futilely, I grabbed the sheet and tried to mop up the blood.

Fists clenched, Bob cried, "We must be doing something wrong."

From the cordless phone I still clutched in one hand, a voice barked, "Is that noise your son?"

"Yes! Yes!"

"Leave him on his side or he'll choke to death."

Within three minutes an ambulance with two paramedics arrived, followed by a fire truck and squad car. I dashed upstairs, let them in, and led the way downstairs.

On the way down I quickly gave the paramedics a review of Mark's bicycle accident 33 hours earlier, his Emergency Room (ER) visit, and the two follow-up medical phone contacts.

Transfixed, Bob and I looked on while paramedics attempted to open Mark's mouth, but his jaws were locked. The team placed a rubber airway in Mark's nose so he wouldn't choke on his blood. They also assisted his breathing using a special mask with a bag. On Mark's neck they placed a brace and wedged sandbags around his head, for immobility.

As we watched, we saw the pupils of Mark's eyes dilating and shifting toward the left. He breathed rapidly, his arms locked across his chest, his legs racked with spasms. Another paramedic took Mark's blood pressure.

Expertly they administered intravenous fluids including glucose, in case of low blood sugar. One paramedic drew blood and administered a medicine we were told would counter a possible drug overdose. To our relief, another team member suctioned mucous and blood from Mark's mouth to prevent the mixture from being drawn into his lungs, causing pneumonia.

They placed our son on a stretcher. As they carried him out, mucous and blood dripped onto the nightstand and floor.

By this time Bob had jerked a pair of trousers on over his pajamas.

"I'll go with Mark," he said.

"I'll follow by car."

Within 12 minutes of their arrival, the paramedics had loaded Mark in the ambulance and sped away, lights flashing.

I dressed hastily and darted out to the driveway. A fireman waited there to tell me they had rushed Mark to the nearest hospital, Providence Medical Center.

Speeding to the hospital, I prayed for Mark, so like his father and all we'd desired in a son.

Thoughts tumbled through my mind. Why had God allowed Mark's bicycle accident? *Why hadn't the clinic nurse listened to my fears about him the day after the accident? Why had the ER doctor suggested Mark's greatest need was rest? Why hadn't I persisted further in getting help for Mark?*

As I raced through empty, early morning streets I was flooded with guilt and bewilderment. *Lord, we don't know anyone at Providence. Oh, God, may we not be too late.*

As I reached the hospital parking lot, my anxiety mounted. Hardly knowing what I did, I parked, got out of the car, and locked it. I darted across the street and ran through Providence's main corridor, where I found the front desk.

"My son, Mark Laughlin, has he been admitted?"

The receptionist nodded, pointing to the ER where I found Bob pacing the floor. For a man who grew faint at the sight of blood, Bob looked well.

Together we slumped onto the couch. "What's happened, Bob?"

Slipping his arm around my shoulder he said, "We sped through red lights-no competition from early morning traffic. I heard one paramedic whisper to his coworker, 'This is the worst case I've ever seen.'"

Blotting that shattering thought out of my mind, I asked, "But, Bob, how's Mark?"

"Mark fought for air. A paramedic rechecked his airway. They reported his history, vital signs, and treatment by radio to the dispatcher, 911 Medical Emergency, and then Providence."

Bob shuddered and his voice trembled as he said, "The shaking of his legs got worse." Nervously snapping his watchband, Bob continued, "Mark's left pupil was huge and seemed unresponsive to light."

I closed my eyes for a moment and buried my head in my hands.

Bob clutched my shoulder and added, "The ambulance staff did a great job right up to the minute they rushed Mark into the emergency room and the doctor took over."

At that point, the attendant from the admitting desk came in and gently interrupted us. She needed Mark's medical history, social security number, and insurance information. We made sure she knew about the medications he couldn't take. Mark had arrived at Providence at 1:10 a.m. The ER physician, Dr. Bonnie Sidoff, confirmed paramedic reports in her initial exam. She told us that our son was in a deep coma.

Later, in a letter, she would tell us the team had administered three drugs to control brain swelling. They also replaced the airway, putting a tube through Mark's nose and throat, into the windpipe, for surer delivery of air. Because Mark's muscles remained rigid, the procedure was difficult and damaged the structures around the windpipe. The staff was concerned about possible infection.

As the clock struck 2:00 a.m., x-ray personnel quickly took Mark for a CT scan. Dr. Michael Markham, the young, on-call neurosurgeon, had arrived and was awaiting the results. Walking briskly into the waiting area, he questioned us about Mark and the events of the past two days.

After Dr. Markham reviewed the x-ray, he informed us that an epidural hematoma (a blood clot between Mark's skull and the covering of his brain) had formed. He asked our permission to relieve the pressure on the brain by drilling a burr hole in Mark's skull. The doctor told us he would drill a hole into the left side of Mark's head and suction blood from the clot, relieving pressure on Mark's brain, a procedure that would take only a few minutes. Bluntly, the doctor told us he had never performed this surgery in such an acute case. Because the area could not be made completely sterile, there were risks of infection. On the other hand, it might save Mark's life so he'd reach the operating table.

Reassured by his candid manner, we consented.

The on-call surgical staff had not arrived, nor was the surgery room ready. At 2:30 a.m. they wheeled Mark from the ER to the 4th floor Intensive Care Unit (ICU) where sufficient staff waited to assist Dr. Markham. After the burr hole was drilled, the orderlies wheeled Mark to the 2nd floor surgery room where the on-call surgical staff prepared our son for surgery.

Dr. Markham told us, "Doing the burr hole bought time but Mark's condition remains critical. I can't give you any assurance that Mark will get off the operating table alive."

"We'll be praying for you and your team."

"We'll need more than prayer."

We wondered whom we should call at 3:00 a.m. Of course, shortly after arriving at the hospital, we had dialed our daughter, Kathy, who lived across town near the medical school, to give her the latest report.

"I'm on my way," she had immediately responded.

Realizing we needed prayer support, we called the Hinson Church college student minister, John Repsold; our associate pastor; and two friends. To our astonishment, a support group of 10, including five of Kathy's friends, arrived within a half-hour and stayed the rest of the night to pray for Mark and us.

In the fourth floor waiting area we gathered around an old, round coffee table laden with magazines and newspapers. We clasped hands and prayed. Bob started, "Oh, God, be with Mark, and if it's your will, spare him." He added, "Help us glorify You in this."

"Accomplish Your will through Mark and his family," John prayed.

"Guide the hands of the surgeon and his assistants," our associate pastor requested.

"Lord, please let my brother be all that he was. Or, in an act of love, take him to be with you."

"Father, Mark's your child," I said. "If it be Your will, bring him back. But, please take him," I stammered, 'if he would not be whole."

As time crawled by we talked and quoted Scripture to each other. We leafed absentmindedly through the table literature, our minds on Mark. Some killed time by drinking coffee. At times I just sat staring at the large, metal-rimmed wall clock.

From time to time, Kathy laid her head on my shoulder and cried softly. I wrapped my arms around her and held her close, sharing my handful of tissues.

When both Kathy and I pleaded with God to take Mark if he wouldn't be normal, I wondered how I could make this request. Then my pain-filled past flashed before me. Throughout my childhood and college years I watched my father fight a losing battle with cancer, frequently dulling his pain in alcohol. Shortly after his death, my mother's prolonged illness was diagnosed as Parkinson's disease. Although she became a bed-ridden invalid for 19 years, Mother modeled faith for me.

I didn't want Mark to experience similar anguish. Even now my mother was helping me look beyond my maternal desires. I longed for Mark to live and resume a normal life, but then I realized anew that Mark was prepared to meet his Creator. I'd see him again.

Meanwhile Kathy, a fourth-year medical student, feared Mark's prognosis. She knew that if her brother lived, the outcome could be grim.

In the early morning hours the hospital seemed to slumber. In the waiting area on Ward 4R, Bob, Kathy, and I, surrounded by friends, waited in near silence. Occasionally calls from a frantic patient echoed in the halls: "Help... Nurse...Help...I'm dying."

Loud, clanging movement in the shaft of the elevator alerted us. Would Mark be coming from surgery? No. Not yet. It was an orderly dashing down the hall. We continued praying, talking, praying, and waiting.

The minutes ticked off the first hour.

During what was left of the night the infrequent movement in the elevator shaft continued as hospital personnel moved from floor to floor.

To be doing something, Kathy and I walked the halls. Anxiously, we wondered about the capabilities of the neurosurgeon.

Rejoining the group, we began reminiscing about Mark. Lynn Wallace, one of Bob's business associates, asked, "How could God allow this accident to happen to such a good kid?"

I paused and swallowed hard. "You just reminded me that today, August 11, is Mark's spiritual birthday. When he was six he sat on my lap and invited Christ into his heart. So simple, but so real."

"You know, Lynn, each year we celebrate the dates Kathy and Mark chose to become Christians. We call these dates their spiritual birthdays."

John cleared his throat. He hesitated and then said, "I've appreciated Mark's faithful help with the college group's activities. He does a great job making visitors feel welcome."

"Including Anne[1]?" I asked.

John smiled. "Definitely Anne. She and Mark make a well-matched twosome. I often wondered when Mark would discover her."

"Should Anne know of Mark's surgery?"

"Yes, and I'll call her."

Awaiting surgery results, however, seemed to be an eternal nightmare. The silence lingered and the suspense grew.

The minutes ticked off the second hour. The surgery continued. We were encouraged that Mark was still alive.

I got up, stretched, and walked the sterile, foreboding corridors again. The sun beaming through the tall, narrow windows at the end of the east-wing hall announced that morning had dawned.

At last our anxious waiting was suddenly interrupted when Dr. Markham stepped off the elevator. Bob, Kathy, and I rushed towards him.

"He's still alive. The brain tissue looks clean and pink." We were overjoyed but then the doctor added, "He may take days, weeks, or even months to wake up. And I have to tell you he may never wake up. It's important that we see signs of consciousness soon."

"Oh, by the way, I'll cancel Mark's doctor appointment," the weary, slump-shouldered doctor said before turning and slowly walking away.

Everyone heard his words. We thanked God. We still had hope. Our friends embraced us and cried with us. Then they assured us of their continued prayers and, one by one, departed.

In a few minutes we saw an orderly wheel Mark into the ICU. The head nurse told us they had instructions for continuous monitoring of his vital signs and brain pressure.

As 7:00 a.m. neared, we knew we needed rest.

Kathy reported Mark's critical status to her instructors and came with us. As we drove home, Bob told Kathy and me that he'd agreed with our prayers, but couldn't voice the words.

Bob called his company, Western Food Equipment (WFE), where he was CEO and informed them of Mark's accident. I called a fellow officer at Stewardship Bank, where I directed marketing, to tell them about Mark and ask for prayer.

---

1.   name changed to protect the identity of a friend.

Shortly after we arrived home, Bob went downstairs. After coming back up he said, "I laid on Mark's bed and trusted him to God's loving care. But in my despair, an epitaph flashed through my mind:

Physical Birth-June 24, 1960

Spiritual Birth-August 11, 1966

With Christ-August 11, 1983"

Then he said, "I'm beat…I'm going to bed."

Kathy and I went down to Mark's disheveled room. Mechanically, we changed the sheets, pillowcases, and mattress cover. Silently, we sponged the mattress and washed the nightstand. We mopped the blood from the floor. Now the bedroom looked neat and tidy, the way Mark kept his space. Drawing a deep breath, I stood back and surveyed the result of our work, determined to be optimistic. "When Mark returns, his room will be ready," I whispered hopefully.

Choked with emotion, Kathy did not say a word but simply walked upstairs and went into the guest bedroom. I could sense what she thought: *Mark will never use his bedroom again.*

Later, while I was making work for myself in the kitchen, the phone's shrill ring startled my already pounding heart. A nurse reported, "Providence needs your consent…"

I wakened Bob. He sprang up from a deep sleep, startled and wild-eyed. A few moments passed before he understood that, in my weariness, I'd failed to tell him our son was still alive. My thoughts had focused on the fact that Mark needed another surgery.

Relaxed, Bob breathed, "All right…Thank you, God. He's alive." He then fell back onto the bed.

I couldn't turn off my spinning mind. Should Mark live, we had a grinding journey ahead. I felt overwhelmed by this impending crisis. *We had promised God to be godly parents, but could we model our faith in this desperate time? Could we influence Mark's recovery? Would the doctors and nurses see anything different in us? How could we honor God before the members of the church where we had belonged for 30 years?*

Jeremiah 9:23,24 reads, "'Let not the wise man boast of his wisdom… but let he who boasts boast about this: that he understands and knows me, that I am the Lord, who exercises kindness, justice, and righteousness on earth, for in these I delight,' declares the Lord."

This passage, which I'd quoted at our last deaconess meeting, tumbled through my mind. Yes, I could confess that I knew God. He delights in kindness, justice, and righteousness, but these truths didn't reflect the present circumstances.

Then again, God's total plan wasn't limited to the hospital's fourth floor on the morning of August 11.

I questioned, but truth needed to rule over my feelings. I knew God could provide peace and strength in the midst of our calamity.

Even though I didn't understand, I could choose to trust God the same way that Mark trusted me throughout his childhood. When I was away from home working in a school office, I could expect the phone to ring and hear a childish voice say, "Hi, Mom. This is Mark. I need somethin'"

Now we were in uncharted waters. The passage was rough and frighteningly unfamiliar. I knew as never before that I needed God's help. I prayed, "Hi, God. This is Milli. Help! Help me. We need Your help"

2

"Hi, Mom. This Is Mark"

○ ○

Grief makes one hour ten.

—*William Shakespeare*

From first grade through his college years, and into his first year of teaching, Mark frequently phoned me. "Hi, Mom. This is Mark."

Sometimes he called just to ask how things were going. His occasional requests seemed reasonable, but urgent in his young mind. Mark was always sure of our support and never doubted our love.

During the years Mark attended grade school I worked in a school office and also taught home economics. I usually arrived home before Mark and Kathy finished their after-school activities. When they arrived home early, Mark called me.

He knew I would chat a moment. "I love ya' and will see ya' soon."

I always welcomed the greeting: "Hi, Mom. This is Mark."

Upon completion of teaching his first year of language arts at Reynolds High School, Mark attended Western Conservative Baptist Seminary (WCBS) the following summer. He took Lifestyle Evangelism, a class on how Christians could more effectively share their faith.

At 4:15 p.m. on August 9, I was buzzed by the receptionist at the bank where I worked.

"Milli speaking."

"Hi, Mom. This is Mark."

His voice sounded strained. "Yes, Mark, is something wrong?"

"I've just had a little bike accident."

Although his voice was unsteady, he assured me he felt okay.

On the day of his accident Mark cycled toward home after registering for the beginning biblical language class, "baby Greek." Two women heard the collision's impact and saw him hurled from his bicycle onto the pavement. They charged across the street. While one assisted Mark into their home, the other placed his bicycle on their porch. They cleaned his scraped left elbow and temple but didn't think he should ride his bicycle home.

Mark insisted I wait until quitting time to pick him up.

"No, Mark, my workday started at 6:30 this morning. I've already put in my time. I'm coming to get you immediately."

"Oh, okay. I'll be waiting."

I thought of Mark's vast cycling experience as I drove. The previous August he had cycled 3,000 miles cross-country to Washington, D.C. with the Judson Baptist College (JBC) cycling group headed by their president, Dr. Herbert Anderson. Their 30-day, educational trip highlighted his summer.

Recently Mark had completed a four-day bicycle trip along the Oregon coast with our church youth group. Besides being a "big-brother" to junior high schoolers, he also led the Bible study.

Mark planned to join another JBC group cycling to Canada on August 11. He would miss one day of seminary class, but had arranged for a make-up session after his return.

Mark had become a capable, expert cyclist who put his heart into this sport.

When I picked up Mark, he looked well, but shaken and favoring his skinned left elbow. He'd ridden his 18-speed bicycle without his helmet, a careless omission that would cause him unimaginable trauma. Distracted by a toe-clip problem, he attempted, but failed, to veer past a parked car. Mark insisted we stop by a bicycle shop to inquire about a handlebar replacement. He wanted to be ready for the early morning take-off from the JBC campus on August 11.

After arriving home we agreed that Mark should rest so he lay down on a deck chair. Uneasily, I reminded myself that Bob would be home soon. We'd eat and then have Mark checked at a hospital ER.

While preparing dinner, I phoned Kathy to tell her about Mark's accident. She suggested that we take him to the Emanuel Hospital ER. Kathy knew of their reputation as a trauma center.

Anne, Mark's special friend, had already planned to visit later in the evening so I did not call her. Bob and I joked with Mark while we ate. Who would drive him to the hospital? We agreed Anne could have the privilege.

Anne and Mark were gone over two hours. Returning from the hospital, Mark reported a crowded ER that required them to wait and wait. "The exams took time, too. But finally the staff x-rayed, checked, and released me," he said.

Mark prepared for sleeping upstairs, in the guest room next to ours, instead of in his own room in the daylight basement. According to the hospital direction sheet, we were to arouse and check him every two hours.

Shortly after midnight I awakened, hearing Mark vomit.

"I have a terrible headache, too."

The information sheet stated we could give him aspirin or Tylenol, but the instructions also said we should report any changes.

Worried, I called Emanuel. "Our son returned from your ER two hours ago. He is vomiting and has a severe headache. What more should we do?"

"He can have aspirin or Tylenol, but don't give him anything stronger," the ER attendant repeated. "That should be enough to quiet him."

We didn't have Tylenol, and Mark was allergic to aspirin. So Bob, therefore, dressed and drove to a convenience store for Tylenol. After our son had taken the medication, he rested better. His headache lessened.

We awakened Mark at regular intervals to check his pupils for size variation and to observe the firmness of his handgrip. Consulting the instructions, we listened for slurred speech and checked for swelling at the temple.

As Mark dressed the next morning he said, "I feel awful. I won't go on the bike trip."

His headache had improved, yet he seemed weary and had no appetite.

Although troubled, I drove to the bank. Bob stayed home to observe Mark and also keep up his normal routine by dictating office memos. To comfort myself, I talked with both Mark and Bob by phone. Before a late lunch, I called our doctor's office.

"Your doctor's nurse will call you in a couple hours."

"No, I need a quicker reply."

The nurse soon returned my call.

"I'd like Mark rechecked." I reported his accident, hospital check, lack of appetite, headache, and continued vomiting.

"We're really busy, and Mark's doctor is out of town. But if he worsens, bring him over. We'll try to work him in somehow. I'll set up an appointment for 9:30 tomorrow morning with one of your doctor's associates."

Although devastated by her response, I reasoned we still had to eat and went home for lunch. I served rice and 7-UP to Mark. He ate very little and continued to lie on the couch. He seemed normal, making several phone calls and talking to two friends who called him. I kept an early afternoon business appointment but returned promptly to monitor Mark.

Besides checking Mark's pupils, handgrip, and mobility, Bob and I tested his coherency. We were relieved that he had remembered to cancel his bicycle trip reservation.

When Mark talked by phone to John, our church's college intern, we didn't notice a lack of recall. But Mark spoke more slowly.

Mark continued to lie listlessly on the couch while Bob and I ate dinner in the living room. Mark sipped more 7-UP, but then rushed into the bathroom to vomit. He came out declaring, "I feel better now."

The three of us spent the evening making conversation and reading. Mark called Anne but, untypically, kept the conversation short.

Mark went to bed around 10 p.m. Bob and I set the alarm for midnight when we would check him again.

Still uneasy, I called Kathy to tell her about her brother's continued symptoms.

"Mom, I'm part of the family. I can't be objective," her voice quivered. "You need outside medical advice."

Even though it was 10:15 p.m., I called the Emanuel ER to report Mark's alarming symptoms to a male voice, probably that of an intern.

"Should we continue awakening Mark?"

"When did the accident occur?"

"Around four yesterday afternoon."

"No. Don't worry. What he needs most is rest".

Based on this advice, Bob turned off the alarm and told Mark we wouldn't need to awaken him during the night.

"In that case, I'll feel much better if I sleep in my own bed," Mark replied.

Within moments I heard Mark vomiting in his bathroom. Unnerved, I rushed downstairs. He was sitting on the bed, smiling.

As he had optimistically claimed earlier, Mark said, "I feel so much better. I'll sleep great." He lay down, pulled up a blanket, and buried his head in a pillow.

Relieved that Mark seemed okay, I went back upstairs. We did not know hemorrhaging had continued and formed a blood clot on the left side of his head between the skull and the covering of his brain.

◆   ◆   ◆

Several hours later, shortly after the surgery, Dr. Fredrick Waller, acting on behalf of Dr. Markham, gave us a stunning report. "A six centimeter blood clot was taken out of your son's skull, the biggest one we've ever removed from a person who lived"–(TBI–traumatic brain injury). Briskly he continued, "He actually has less than a one percent chance of living through the day." Almost as an afterthought, he concluded with a hammer blow. "If Mark lives, he will be greatly impaired, mentally and physically."

The ER records revealed that, on the Glascow Coma Scale, ranging from 3 (no responses) to 15 (normal responses), Mark scored a 4. He had no eye response, no verbal response, and only involuntary movements of the arms and legs.

How could this have happened before our eyes? Surely this trauma would pass.

It didn't.

This chilling drama one might witness on the news, a disaster that occurred to others. But a crushing blow like this could never happen to one in your own family.

Yet, it had. How quickly our perception of life changed.

I knew God was all-knowing, all-powerful, and His presence was everywhere. Why had He allowed this tragedy?

Searching for comfort, I remembered a verse I learned as a child: "As for God, his way is perfect; the word of the Lord is flawless. He is a shield for all who take refuge in him" (Ps. 18:30).

But medically speaking, being a TBI victim meant Mark most likely would never walk, talk, feed himself and would require 24-hour nursing care. Words were not adequate to express the fear that gripped me. Everything seemed out of control. However, I tried to tell myself, *God knows. God cares. God allowed the accident for a purpose. What purpose I can't understand.*

The struggle deepened, yet I forced myself to complete several household tasks, call our immediate family members, and cancel business appointments before we left to visit Mark.

3

Doubting In The Dark

○ ○

In order to realize the worth of the anchor, we need to feel the stress of the storm.

—Author unknown

Weary and apprehensive, we returned to the hospital. The news of Mark's accident and surgeries had spread. Over 100 families involved with our church prayer tree had been asked to pray. Bob's sister in Astoria, Oregon, called to report, "I've called eight churches. Their prayer chain members are praying for Mark."

The receptionist's desk near the ICU was inundated with messages of love and concern for Mark and our family. Bob kept accepting and returning calls. A care basket, filled with nutritious food, was delivered to us by our Church Administrator's family. As was allowed, we visited Mark every half hour, two at a time, to stay for the permitted two minutes.

Mark's trim, bronze body, strung with tubes and wires, looked mechanical and unbalanced. They had shaved the wavy blond hair only on the left side of his head. Intravenous feedings of fluids and glucose were administered and a tube down his windpipe connected to a ventilator assisted his breathing. "This tube in the skull," Kathy explained, "siphons off excess fluid."

Having had family members critically ill before, Bob and I were not strangers to hospital settings. But we did appreciate Kathy's assistance in interpreting Mark's vital signs, including his intracranial pressure and heart rate, which registered on a monitor.

She told us that the body temperature of a brain-damaged patient is crucial since the brain is the temperature regulator. The brain's need for oxygen goes up as the body temperature increases. A slight fever, therefore, can make the difference between healing and lack of recovery.

"The continuous monitoring of Mark's intracranial pressure measures the amount of swelling," Kathy stated. "This measurement is critical for the first 72 hours. Further brain swelling can cause additional brain damage." She paused before adding,"...or even death."

She concluded, "An injured brain may show abnormal electrical impulse activity. The anticonvulsant being administered to Mark intravenously will prevent such seizures."

An indwelling urinary catheter provided drainage. Mark's legs postured (moved involuntarily), indicating serious head injury. Since the left side of the brain had greater damage, the right leg vibrated more than the left.

Mark ran a fever and great beads of sweat rolled from his forehead. A large fan on high speed directed an air current the full length of his body.

We knew an unresponsive patient's sense of hearing might still be functioning. We went in to see Mark, talked to him, and kissed his forehead.

"You have excellent care, Mark. We love you."

Bob quoted the 23rd Psalm: "The Lord is my shepherd"...and I, knowing that Mark could find comfort in Psalm 121, recited, "I will lift up my eyes unto the hills. From whence cometh my help? My help cometh from the Lord who made heaven and earth." As we prayed we gently squeezed his hands. Our two minutes flashed by. Assuring him we'd be back soon, we departed.

In the late morning Dr. Markham told us, "Mark's still unresponsive to all stimuli. He also has an injured brain stem so he can't swallow. But he's in excellent physical condition and hasn't harmed his body with drugs."

In between our two-minute visits, our friends met with us in the waiting area. They embraced us, wept with us, and prayed with us. Talking with others about the accident and the following events gave some relief from our constant emotional stress.

More than once I felt encouraged by the slight movement of Mark's arms.

Kathy countered, "Mom, those are involuntary reflexes." She gently placed her hand on my shoulder. "Mark shows no voluntary responses."

How quickly the years had vanished since Kathy played doctor and nurse roles as a child. While a teenager, she supported hurting friends, worked as a candy striper in a hospital, and bagged blood for the Red Cross. She then plunged into her pre-med studies.

Oregon Health Science University (OHSU), where Kathy's medical training began, had also challenged her once child-like faith. She understood and shared doubts voiced by the medical team. God's power to heal was being overshadowed by her medical knowledge. No words could express the shock and confusion reflected in her eyes as her brother feverishly struggled. Bravely he fought for life as she helplessly watched.

We had no real controls, but self-appointed tasks allowed each of us limited control in our uncontrollable situation. The hospital had become so deluged with phone calls for us that the fourth-floor receptionists were frazzled. Bob started taking care of those calls and kept one of his office staff informed about developments. He also left his office number at the receptionist's desk. When he couldn't be located, his office could be called for an up-to-date report.

Through Kathy's connections at OHSU, where she was in her final year, she learned that Dr. Markham was considered one of the top neurosurgeons in Oregon. We thanked God for the physician He'd chosen for Mark.

One of the callers I spoke with identified himself as an acquaintance of Mark's who had also once been in a coma.

"Will you pull the plug if he doesn't snap out of it in 30 days?"

For a moment I couldn't believe what I had heard. After an awkward pause I said quietly, "God asks us to take life one moment at a time. That's where I am."

I thanked him for his concern but his tactlessness angered me. Fortunately, journaling helped purge my rage. Between ICU visits, coping with visitors, and consultations, I found release by recording our emotional agony.

My journaling also brought back another critical time in our lives. Shortly after Bob and I were married, I had a thyroid cancer removed. The doctor informed us I would probably live two and one-half years, possibly up to 15. He advised us never to have children. Yet, Bob and I hoped God would allow us to start a family, promising Him we would rear our children for His glory.

Our dilemma drew us nearer to God, and Proverbs 3:5,6 became our life verses: "Trust in the Lord with all your heart and lean not on your own understanding; in all your ways acknowledge him, and he will make your paths straight."

Strengthened, Bob and I waited two and one-half years before considering parenthood. We counseled with our pastor and a Christian doctor who both encouraged us to walk by faith. We prayed about our children before conception and we prayed for them before birth. We prayed they would commit themselves to their Creator, glorifying Him throughout their lives.

Bob and I told our children not only that they were gifts from God, but that God had gifted them. He would require much. They set high standards for themselves.

After Mark's accident a Providence psychology intern, studying for his doctorate, approached us to say he appreciated knowing Mark through our church youth group. "In my opinion, Mark truly is a caring person. He reaches out to those who need to know someone loves them. You don't usually speak this way about a fella', but I mean it in the most positive way: I think Mark is the sweetest guy I've ever met."

His comments made me remember our son's actions when I had been ill. My chronic depression finally yielded after seven years of trying to find the right thyroid hormone replacement. For my children I was a working mother who was always tired. As a second grader, Mark had won a prize memorizing verses at Bible club. He had a number of items from which to choose. "Mom, I hope you feel better soon." He handed me a tiny flower vase that he had selected as his prize.

The day Mark graduated as salutatorian of his college class, the four of us dined at a restaurant near the school. Mark had sat quietly for some time, and then asked Bob if he remembered when they started jogging together. "When I was in first grade I asked you, 'Am I retarded?'"

"I don't remember your question. But did I convince you that you weren't?"

"You sure did and was I relieved." After a pause Mark added, "The other kids laughed when I read."

I then said, "Mark when you started first grade your teacher wanted you retested. You couldn't pronounce your R's. But the speech therapist said you remained within the norm and would become a stuttering child unless you were left alone. Our concerns relieved, we stopped your word pronunciation exercises and your speech problem disappeared."

Throughout childhood and adolescence, Mark displayed an interest in our missionary friends and asked questions about their purposeful lives. Bob and I rejoiced when our 23 year-old son told us he planned to enroll in the seminary missions program. We were sure Mark was acting in God's will.

Why then, minutes after Mark confirmed his commitment by seminary registration, had God allowed our son's immediate plans to be overruled?

Had we misunderstood God? Was it human error on Mark's part? How could God be glorified through Mark's death or catastrophic insult?

The event baffled us. However, we didn't question the rightness of God's acts. We believed that God, too, experienced pain in Mark's accident.

For the past 30 years we had lived by Proverbs 3:5,6. We gave testimony to His goodness. God had brought us through deep crises. He had granted me life beyond medical predictions. We knew, no matter how we felt, that now was no time to doubt Him.

◆   ◆   ◆

Mark had survived the first 15 hours. On that first day every minute became a bonus. But could they stabilize the brain swelling? Could he weather the critical period of the next two and one-half days when swelling most often occurs?

As I pondered these questions, Dr. Markham came by on evening rounds. Bob asked, "How's Mark doing?"

"He responded slightly to deep pain. This is an excellent sign."

I then believed God would give Mark back to us.

We arrived home late. Having had little sleep for 48 hours, Bob and I went to bed. Wrapped in each other's arms, we wept and prayed that God would heal Mark. We prayed that we would be a testimony to others and thanked God for all who supported us. But falling asleep was difficult.

Back at the hospital on the second day, however, Mark showed no response.

"Maybe we were four hours too late," said Dr. Markham, shaking his head. "I have to tell you that, if he lives, he most likely will be greatly impaired."

Those abrasive words, like a black dagger, sank into my heart. Crushed, I could say nothing while Dr. Markham, looking defeated, turned and left with a heavy stride. I sensed his great distress.

I reminded myself not to rely on medical counsel alone. In the face of all contradictions, my faith had to be placed in God.

On the third evening Mark's special friend, Anne, came to the hospital. While we waited for Bob to arrive from work, she, Kathy, and I talked. Kathy explained Mark's coma and his alarmingly lifeless-seeming body, and described all the ICU equipment to which he was attached. "Are you sure you want to see Mark?" I asked.

"I do," Anne replied.

We agreed that Kathy should accompany Anne because our daughter could explain Mark's care from a doctor's point of view. After their visit with Mark, Kathy took me aside. "She has a charming, quiet manner. I can tell she really cares for Mark."

Later, Kathy mused, "May Mark get completely well so he can marry that beautiful girl."

The next day being Sunday, we visited Mark on our way to early church. He remained in critical condition, but the brain pressure was stable. Our associate pastor announced Mark's grave condition at the beginning of the early service. He told us he would do the same at the later service. Each time our congregation of friends was asked to pray for Mark. The emotion-packed morning drained me; I had difficulty singing. My vision blurred, words began swimming, and I could barely swallow over the lump in my throat.

After the service we went to our usual Philathian Sunday school class where Bob was asked to speak about Mark. He realized how stunned they were and knew what they needed to hear. Firmly, he declared, "We believe Mark is under the care of the Great Physician. With us, trust God for a miracle."

◆　　　◆　　　◆

While we were at church one of the surgeons completed a vital surgical procedure by making a small incision in Mark's windpipe. Into the opening he inserted a breathing tube which was attached to a respirator to supply humidified air to his lungs more directly than the one inserted through his nose. Through this opening (tracheostomy), therapists suctioned Mark's lungs to help protect him from pneumonia.

When we came back to the fourth floor we learned that Mark's condition remained critical. Dr. Markham then said, "You need to get away from this emotion-packed setting. Often when a patient gets better, emotionally exhausted family members don't have enough energy to assist. Pace yourselves," he added before striding down the hall.

We were still thinking about his advice when Anne stepped off the elevator to give me a big hug. In return, I gave her the pictures of Mark she'd requested.

Bob invited Anne to go in for the two-minute visit with Mark. When she came out she said quietly, "Mom and Dad Laughlin, I'll be praying for you," and then departed for Salem to visit her parents.

Now, in addition to spiritual support from relatives and friends, we began hearing from people we didn't know. The love of God shining through anyone who loved Him supplied the strength we needed.

One comforting note came from the Assistant to the Registrar at WCBS. "You don't know me," she stated, "but I met Mark just minutes before the accident as he registered for fall term." She promised to pray for his total recovery. "I was very much impressed with his evident character. What a fine young man Mark is. May our Savior convince you He does love you very much".

Meanwhile, although Mark's condition was critical, the brain swelling remained stable. We learned, now, that his body temperature had also stabilized. The immediate danger of death had passed. Our son, therefore, would be moved to the acute care unit.

In anticipation of the transfer I penned in my journal on <u>SUNDAY, AUGUST 14:</u>

> Thank you, God, that Mark's life is no longer in great danger. But he may never be anything more than a vegetable. That'd be torture! How can we bear this constant pain?
>
> Lord, provide us some relief.
>
> I must also mention that Paul Fleischmann (Mark's most significant mentor) stopped by again. He asked, "Milli, do you remember my being here the first day?" I said, "Yes, Paul, I do, but don't remember a thing that was said." He replied, "No words were spoken, I just wrapped you in my arms and we wept."

4

Promises In The Light

○ ○

Doubt makes the mountain which faith can move.

—Author unknown

I continued to record my helplessness and hurt:

MONDAY, AUGUST 15

My heart is full. I've much to record. Most importantly, Mark is out of ICU! They've transferred him to a private room in the Acute Care Unit near the nurses' station.

I was too excited to sleep. Who wouldn't be? I arrived early to decorate Mark's room with colorful posters, get-well cards, and potted plants. On the wall at the foot of his bed, where he can see it when he wakes up, I placed a poster:

God is the blessed controller of all things I TIMOTHY 6:15

23

As though confirming the thought, here came Mark on a gurney, still in a coma, accompanied by orderlies. That starchy head nurse asked me to wait in the hall. They had to shift Mark to his bed and hook him up to an assortment of machinery. When I went back in, the nurse introduced herself while standing next to Mark's bed. After explaining the room set-up, she said, "His vital signs are being monitored. We'll keep a close check on your son."

She went on educating me. "Mark is wearing support hose to help prevent blood clots. In addition, he'll be turned from his back to his side every two hours; this will improve his circulation and protect him from bedsores. Turning will also help prevent pneumonia or other infection from settling in his lungs."

While she talked in her brisk, matter-of-fact manner, I wiped Mark's forehead and adjusted his pillow. "This tube inserted through Mark's nose goes into his stomach. It provides for feedings given every three hours. Also, frequent blood samples will be drawn. Mark will wear foot braces, extending to his knees, to help prevent contractures (ankle drops). These will be worn for two hours and taken off for two hours. As you can see," the nurse said while pointing, "Mark's right foot no longer forms a right angle to his leg."

She paused, and then seemed to speak louder. "How terrible! What a shame! Such a promising young man."

Before she could continue, I blurted, "Mark doesn't need to hear this."

There was an awkward silence. She looked startled and bewildered. "Thanks anyway," I stammered.

Still staring, she left.

I then sat by Mark's bedside, wiped his forehead again, and rubbed his arms to tell him I was there. I told him that I loved him and that he must keep fighting.

As I jot these notes, tears wet my journal. I fear Mark's potentials are lost.

◆   ◆   ◆

Bob and I decided returning to work was our best coping therapy. Forcing myself, I drove to the bank. I passed a note among my associates saying I was too emotionally fragile to cope with sympathy.

I drove to two business contacts, but my thoughts were never far from Mark. On the second call, distracted, I left my keys in the ignition, locking myself out. Thanks to the American Automobile Association's (AAA) rescue, I drove back to the bank.

After work I read and prayed with Mark, glad I could stay longer now, and greeted friends until visiting hours ended. Still, he lay as though lifeless.

Mary Ann Zimmerman, a nurse practitioner and mother of three preschoolers, offered to give me a daily back rub. She was my angel from heaven.

MONDAY, AUGUST 15 (Cont.)

I drove home in a weary daze, heading for bed. But, Lord, please don't let me step off course. I want to finish the race well. I hope Mark's accident will bring Bob and me into a closer relationship. Thank You that Bob never wavers in his belief that Mark will be healed. His optimistic nature helps me keep going.

TUESDAY, AUGUST 16

When I visited Mark this morning, I was thrilled he remained stable. But, Lord, will he ever wake up?

When I arrived at the bank I found a message from the Business Manager at Reynolds High School where Mark taught last year. She said Mark had forgotten to sign a medical waiver.

Thank You, God, that Mark has medical coverage!

When the school receives Mark's payment, he will be covered under Reynolds' medical plan for another six months. After that he'll be switched to an individual plan with fewer benefits. We'll deal with that later.

I was anxious to know how Mark was doing and rushed to the hospital at the end of the workday. Although a rash still covered Mark's body, there was good news, too:

- his legs no longer vibrate;

- his temperature remains constant;

- once his right eye opened slightly; and

- Bob thinks he observed some eye movement (tracking) earlier.

Thank you, God, for these good signs.

◆   ◆   ◆

When Bob arrived we hung a kite from the ceiling. I treasured this creation Mark had designed and stitched for me the previous Christmas. I felt Mark would enjoy watching the flight of his handiwork and its warm, earthy colors livened his room.

I placed cut flowers and plants where they could be seen and enjoyed by Mark. I opened and read to our son the stack of cards and letters he'd received. One special note stated: "So many, many people are asking how you are, Mark. They are praying for you and your dear family...We're asking for and expecting a miracle!"

Visitors stopped by and Bob intercepted them at the door and asked that they only speak words of encouragement. He invited them to sit and talk to Mark.

"When you say something to Mark, assume he understands. Touch him, if you feel comfortable doing that. Also, please make statements rather than asking questions."

WEDNESDAY, AUGUST 17

Another stressful morning visit. Mark's mechanical supports and remoteness hurt me. They told me he remains stable without change. Even so, the day had some pluses.

Ted Bailey, a person Mark had worked with, came into the bank to transact business with a teller. After that, he approached my desk, slumped into a chair, and sat with his head in his hands. I knew he was thinking about Mark.

"Milli, I'm so sorry. I don't know what to say. How could this happen to Mark? He's such a great guy." I told him I felt crushed and wrung out, but that God was in control. "If Mark dies I know I'll see him again and that comforts me."

I could see how intently he was now listening. I paused, breathed deeply, moistened my lips and, prodded from within, continued, "Ted, do you know where you'd go if you died tonight?"

"Uh, not really..."

"Would you like to know?"

When Ted looked up and said so simply, "Sure," I felt my eyes fill with tears.

From a desk drawer, I took out my small Bible, hesitated, and swallowed hard. Ted moved his chair closer and leaned forward. I knew at that moment he was ready to hear John 3:16 and John 10:10.

"Ted, can you believe that Christ is the Son of God?"

"Yes, because I was taught that in parochial school."

I said, "Romans 3:23 and 6:23 tell us we are sinful. Ted, do you believe that you're a sinner?"

"I sure am."

I could hardly believe how ready he was, but went on to explain God's remedy for sin in John 5:8 and Ephesians 2:8,9 where we are told salvation is a gift.

I laid my hand on his and told him, "Ted, salvation is free."

His face lit up. "That's so simple."

As we bowed our heads, Ted prayed simply, asking for forgiveness for his sins. He invited Christ to control his life. I thanked God for Ted's decision.

"Ted, remember this date. It's your spiritual birthday."

I sighed and then smiled as we stood up and embraced.

"I know you're in deep pain," Ted said in a quivering voice, "but thanks for caring about me." He then turned and slowly walked away.

Out of this blackness there is some light.

◆   ◆   ◆

When I arrived at the hospital, I learned that Mark was able to swallow. This very significant improvement encouraged me. I bent over and hugged his stiff body. Then I sat down by his side and gripped his hand.

"Mark, I led Ted Bailey to the Lord today. Your accident made him think." I was sure Mark understood even though he didn't respond.

Dr. Markham cautioned us, "Mark needs lots of stimulation, so keep on being here for him."

Bob stayed at the hospital a short time before leaving for a deacons' meeting at church. When he came home he was glowing with hope. He said, "I'm overjoyed by the prayers of our church staff and deacon board. We knelt for nearly an hour asking that, if it be God's perfect will, He would restore Mark."

THURSDAY, AUGUST 18

No visible change in Mark this morning, but our beloved pastor, Don Baker (hereafter called Pastor), and deacons came to pray for him.

Pastor walked onto the fourth floor and embraced us. "How's Mark and how are you two holding up?"

"Mark is stable and God is meeting our needs," Bob said.

When the nine deacons and church staff arrived we gathered around Mark's bed and Pastor said, "Bob, Milli, and Kathy desire to act upon James 5:14 and 15. 'Is any one of you sick? He should call the elders of the church to pray over him and anoint him with oil in the name of the Lord. And the prayer offered in faith will make the sick person well; the Lord will raise him up. If he has sinned, he will be forgiven.'" Pastor read the passage and then anointed Mark with oil before everyone, packed with emotion, prayed.

We are receiving calls from Anne. Mark and Anne's relationship has been a casual, refreshing one. Her character impresses me.

Dare I believe that some day they will marry?

But right now Mark is our priority. Lord, nothing else matters.

◆   ◆   ◆

Dr. Markham had taken Mark off the anticonvulsant, Dilantin, because of the side effect-the massive rash-and put him on a different anti-seizure drug.

Another problem, the humidified air that escaped from the respirator, steamed Mark's face making him look as though he had acute adolescent acne. Through all this Mark's basic condition remained critical. His eyes, although often vacant and glassy, focused intermittently, the right eye opening wider than the left eye.

FRIDAY, AUGUST 19

Because of her medical knowledge Kathy recognizes the seriousness of Mark's accident. She's in agony. I'm aware she can't tell us how critical his prognosis is.

Our dear daughter hides her fear and visits Mark each afternoon after classes. For the first time in her medical training she has taken fewer courses during the summer. Could she have sensed somehow that God was helping her make room to be with Mark? Will this help her faith? I believe that lighter load is a signal for her.

Hold me close, Lord. I'm emotionally spent and weak. Give me Your strength.

SATURDAY, AUGUST 20

I arrived early to visit Mark. I rubbed and rotated his arms. I quoted Psalms 23 and 121, probably more for my comfort than his. I wondered, Lord, he does hear me, doesn't he?

I gazed at the walls full of get-well cards, but again and again my eyes were drawn to the poster at the foot of Mark's bed: "GOD IS THE BLESSED CONTROLLER OF ALL THINGS."

Do I believe these words? My feelings do not affirm this statement. This truth doesn't erase the pain I feel that goes on and on.

While sitting at Mark's bedside, I remembered that I had with me sermon notes from a recent series Pastor preached on Job. He said, "Before any calamity reached Job, it had to have the permission of God. Sometimes the only answer is God allows suffering. He is in complete control."

But, can we put into practice the Biblical principles we've been taught? We want to make a positive statement to the watching world. Yet we face an awesome task. For years we have known and taught Biblical truths. We practiced what we believed. Can we now display these concepts in our critical situation, allowing Truth to guide us?

The challenge overwhelms me. With your help, Lord, we ask for strength to meet Your test. I can't however, dispel the fear of faltering.

◆   ◆   ◆

As Kathy and I shared our fears with each other, her presence gave me comfort. We began asking each other the tough questions.

"Why didn't I have Mark checked despite our clinic being 'too busy?'"

She countered with, "Why didn't I take Mark's situation seriously sooner?"

"Why hadn't I had Mark rechecked at the ER although they'd advised me to let him sleep?"

Kathy cried out, "Why did God allow this to happen to my brother?"

"Why" was our constant cry. We struggled for relief that came slowly as we gave up guilt and agreed that God was sovereign.

We wanted to more than survive this crisis. Through our painful experience we wanted to learn and grow.

While at the hospital, my two sisters, their husbands, and a nephew from out of town walked in, surprising us because they came so far and unexpectedly. As we embraced, our emotions left us speechless. Their stunned expressions reflected their horror and distress as they saw Mark's lifeless-like, wasting body hooked up to so much apparatus.

Mark's flood of company continued. My sisters and I walked down the hall to make room for other visitors.

A nurse rushed toward me. "Mrs. Laughlin, you'll probably not like what I have to say. Mark has entirely too much company. He needs time to rest."

"Thanks, I feel the same way. Dr. Markham told us Mark needs lots of stimulation, but I don't think he has any idea how many friends and relatives traffic in and out of his room."

Promptly the nurses posted a sign on Mark's door:

Please Limit visitors

to <u>two</u> at a time!

<u>10 minute</u> intervals.

<u>Mark needs rest time</u>

Any questions check at Nursing station.

I also posted on the 4R18 door another sign which my friend, Ruth Ann Tidswell, had had made:

Everything said in here must be positive

As I went to bed that evening that sign reminded me of the day Mark invited one of his high school English students, Duane Brown, to be interviewed in the seminary class on "Lifestyle Evangelism." This was the day before Mark's accident. As I drifted off to sleep, I wondered what effect Mark's experience would have on Duane.

5

Seed Bears Fruit

o o o o o o o o o o o o o o o o o o o o o o o o o o o o o o o o

The salvation of a soul isn't a solo; it's a symphony.
—Michael Guido with Sarah Coleman

When we stopped by the hospital before going to church, I thought Mark tracked our movements. "Good job, Mark." I gave him a big hug.

In our Sunday school class Bob presented an update on Mark. In conclusion he said, "We pray the medical staff will confirm Mark's eyes are tracking."

SUNDAY, AUGUST 21

This morning I struggled with my emotions in our Sunday school class. It didn't help to be ignored by a friend who came in late, sat next to me, and left quickly after the session. How cruel. I felt like I was contagious. Maybe she didn't know how to handle our crisis. I couldn't cope with sympathy, but being slighted shredded my emotions, too. I needed affirmation.

Mark tracked periodically throughout the afternoon. However, most of the time he appeared to be in a restless sleep. His stomach must have been churning since his breath was so rotten. I hope he's not in physical pain and mental anguish, too.

Dreams shattered. Hopes dashed. Will life ever be the same again? I feel I'm in a tunnel with no light. But help me, God, to have enduring faith.

◆   ◆   ◆

Around noon Mark's seminary professor came in to the bank.

"You have a fine son and all the school is praying for Mark daily," he told me. "He showed Duane Brown how to become a member of God's family. Duane didn't make a decision for Christ, but he's interested. Do you want to call him?"

"I'll need to think about that," I responded.

"Here's a script of that session that was videoed. You'll be pleased with Mark's commendable presentation. Be assured of our prayers."

That evening as I sat beside Mark's bedside I thought back to early summer when Mark deepened a relationship with an unbeliever for the Lifestyle Evangelism class assignment. He and Duane, one of his former English students, went water-skiing. When Mark explained that he had a special assignment to interview someone before the seminary class, Duane had agreed.

The day before the accident, Mark took Duane to class and explained how God could become an important part of his life.

Now, here I was reading the 10-page interview dialogue while seated at Mark's bedside, the accident a terrible reality. I put the script aside frequently so that I could regain my composure. Although any awareness on Mark's part would have been welcome, I didn't want him to see me crying.

Mark's depth of faith and his sensitive ability to simply express his trust in God helped him to masterfully communicate God's love to Duane.

Mark began the interview session in front of the class by saying, "Duane was in my language arts class last year, but later I felt a need to get out of education. It wasn't the most important thing in the world to me. Verbs and adjectives are handy tools when you want to communicate with someone, but if they're the most important things in your life, you've got some problems. "That's why I'm in seminary. My priorities have changed."

Toward the end of the dialogue Mark turned toward Duane. "I wanted to present these ideas to you, and give you this sketched diagram of the relationship between God and man and have you think about it. As I said before, it's the most important thing in my life.

"You should make a decision so that you can be sure, if you died, you'd go to heaven. It is something that can happen at any minute..."

"As I've come to know more about God, it seems I've come to give more of myself to him. Maybe that's because I've begun to recognize what He's done for me"...

Duane was silent for a moment. "I think I understand, but I need time to think."

"Mark, will you close in prayer?" the instructor asked.

"Father, I thank you that Duane and I crossed paths. As I look back on teaching, I wonder about the value of that experience. But if it includes the chance to know Duane better, to introduce him to You, that will be profit enough. God, I pray in the time that Duane and I share this afternoon and in the contacts we'll have in the future, we'll be able to clarify his ideas of You and his relationship with You…I ask these things in your Son's name, Amen."

Lord, how can I understand why Mark's promising future has been derailed or possibly destroyed? It doesn't seem fair.

MONDAY, AUGUST 22

My angel nurse, Mary Ann, comes daily. For a few moments I forget our nightmare as she massages my neck and back. I know these precious moments are an important break from the reality of life. She is one of your faithful servants, Lord, and I thank You for her.

TUESDAY, AUGUST 23

Progress! There are signs of Mark's sight and hearing. The nursing staff reported some tracking of his eyes. "The left eye opens slightly while the right eye at times opens normally. Mark also responds to following a light on command," the head nurse said.

The Hinson college department has rallied, acting upon 1 Thessalonians 5:17: "Pray continually." They've organized a twenty-four hour prayer chain. Dave Wahlstrom, a college roommate of Mark's, visits Mark daily and keeps the 110-member group informed.

I still feel an inner prodding from You, Lord, to call Duane, introduce myself, and make an appointment for a luncheon.

I'm torn by my emotions. Can I handle the trauma?

A part of me says, "Don't be naive; you'll make a blubbering spectacle of yourself." On the other hand, I countered, "You can't accomplish this in your own strength."

Another voice said, "Trust me, child."

◆   ◆   ◆

Finally I dialed Duane's number. When he answered the phone I introduced myself and invited him to lunch. He accepted and we set a luncheon date for the next day.

TUESDAY, AUGUST 23 (Cont.)

Cards, letters, phone calls, and telegrams keep flowing in with affirming messages. But I'm rebuked because I haven't understood why my friend avoided me on Sunday. She wrote these undeserved words that I must record:

"Sitting next to you yesterday in SS class made me aware of your lives in a special way. The strength of your character and the personal God you display. The reality of God is wonderful to see and it renewed my faith, which has been sagging lately.

"We do pray for a miracle in raising Mark up from the coma. He exemplifies all that one could wish for in a son."

Lord, help me keep my self-talk positive. What I think and do in private is my true character that only You and I know. I want my character to match my reputation, but I fear they are drifting further and further apart.

◆   ◆   ◆

Coma therapy began with Mark scheduled for speech, physical, and occupational therapy from 8:00 a.m. through 4:00 p.m. He had an extended noon break that allowed time for tube feeding and rest.

WEDNESDAY, AUGUST 24

When leaving the hospital just before noon, I told Mark that I was having lunch with Duane, even though I wondered if he understood me. During lunch Duane said, "Mr. Laughlin knows his Bible and is sure of his future. He's convincing." That was the cue I needed.

With moist hands and a tight throat, I told Duane that Mark would consider it worthwhile if giving his life would result in Duane's decision for Christ. My voice cracked. After a prolonged pause I apologized.

"Uh, that's okay," he said. Like a bud bursting into bloom, he accepted Christ. In all my frailty, God used me.

What childlike faith Duane showed when he stepped into Your family. Lord, there's no greater thrill than being used as a vessel to bring someone to You. I'm thankful for that privilege.

But, Lord, this evening Mark appeared exhausted. I'm crushed that he couldn't share my excitement about Duane. I think his coma therapy did him in. I wonder will he ever come out of it? If so, when?

But, thank You, Lord, prayers are being answered.

6

Complications

Prayer is the highest use to which speech can be put.

—*P. T. Forsyth*

During daily visits with Mark, I observed his therapists giving him physical and occupational range-of-motion exercises. Later, twice a day, I would perform these passive movements with his arms, hands, legs, and feet.

Meanwhile, Kathy faithfully maintained her bedside vigil until I arrived after work. The doctors, Bob, and I told her she should take a break, but she remained at Mark's side.

"Mark, this is Kathy," she said as she squeezed her brother's hand and wiped his feverish brow. "You're making progress. I'll spend the afternoon with you. I believe you know that you're at Providence Hospital and receiving excellent care. All your needs are being met."

As she rubbed Mark's arms, Kathy added, "You need rest so you'll continue healing. I'll read to you now."

THURSDAY, AUGUST 25

Daily, as I watch Kathy's bedside manner, I observe the ideal doctor. She treats the whole person, displaying loving care. Sometimes Kathy has reddened eyes when I relieve her. Although often exhausted, she never complains. She is a stabilizer and a comforter for Bob and me even though she, too, is in shock.

35

THURSDAY, AUGUST 25 (Cont.)

It was so wonderful getting a hug from Anne. Oh, how I've missed her. We both are excited because we believe Mark recognized her voice when she greeted him. Lord, I know he did, didn't he?

Yet, it's dreadfully painful watching Mark struggle and now he has a bladder infection. It seems life is out of focus. Please, Lord, may there be no more complications.

◆   ◆   ◆

I had a fitful sleep, but was relieved this morning when Dr. Markham told us that the urinary infection had lessened. "I'm stopping the second anticonvulsant, Phenobarbital, because the medication drugs Mark too much. He may have seizures," he said, "but they won't hurt him." He paused, and then added, "It's great to see some intermittent eye tracking. Mark will fight back because of his excellent physical condition and youth."

I cherished these words from our doctor who had previously prophesied nothing but gloom.

After Dr. Markham's departure Kathy said, "Mom, Mark may need medication for seizures all his life.'"

"Kathy, I can't accept that now. If he can't handle these drugs, God will see that he doesn't need them."

FRIDAY, AUGUST 26

Yet another painful hurdle. The nurses report Mark has high blood pressure. Lord, provide for Mark what the doctors cannot.

SATURDAY, AUGUST 27

A great start today. The urinary infection is gone. Some of our prayers have been answered.

Bob and I discussed how oily and unkempt Mark's hair had become after 17 days in the hospital. I had brought clippers and a special crew-cut blade. Bob turned Mark's head slowly as I cut the hair on the right side of his head to match the stubble on the left.

Looking up, I saw that Bob was tense and pale. That did it. My hands started shaking. "We need a break," I said. Our emotions had collapsed. A short time later, after we had breathed deeply and regained control, we continued.

Bob turned Mark onto his left side and we braced him with pillows. Then Bob held Mark's head off the pillow while I cut the hair on the back of his head. Mark's physical appearance had improved, but how pale and gaunt he looked. Yet his blondish-auburn beard had grown in thick. Not once did our son show any sign of awareness. The eerie task, as if preparing a corpse for a funeral, left us emotionally wrenched.

While I walked up and down the corridors to relax, Bob remained somewhat composed and stayed by Mark's side, his silence and saddened look revealing his unspoken anguish. It hurt so to be touching Mark but getting no smiles, no hugs, no response of any kind. In addition to his high blood pressure, Mark now had a cough. What next?

SUNDAY, AUGUST 28

On our before-church visit we learned that Mark's cough had worsened into a tracheal infection. He received two antibiotics and the respiratory therapists were regularly suctioning his lungs. Knowing this was painful for Mark, watching the procedure hurt me, too. I left.

◆   ◆   ◆

When Dr. Anderson, Mark's intended cycling partner, returned from the 17 day Canadian bicycle excursion, he and his wife immediately visited Mark. In our evening church service, where Dr. Anderson was guest speaker, he paid tribute to our son's cycling and expressed his tender concern for Mark's welfare.

After evening church we returned to the hospital. Periodically Mark would open his eyes, looking distressed. He appeared to be pleading for relief.

Because Mark remained distraught and tense, I didn't complete the passive exercises. In addition to the infection, his blood pressure had soared to 250/150.

SUNDAY, AUGUST 28 (Cont.)

I cling to the Biblical truth in Psalms 147:3: "He heals the brokenhearted and binds up their wounds." I repeat a prayer I had memorized: "Heavenly Father, watch over Your child. Grant that Mark may be restored to perfect health that is Yours alone to give. May You delight in healing Mark because of Your loving kindness toward those who are praying."

After kissing Mark good night I cried all the way home. God, You know I pleaded with You. I'm helpless. I can't help Mark in any way. I feel part of me is dying on that hospital bed. I hurt so, God. I'm angry.

But in the midst of my outpour, Lord, You calmed me. I was reminded that the One You loved faced death, too. You watched Your son experience the torment of scourging, degradation, humiliation, and death. That was the reason You came to earth to bear the sin of all mankind.

God, are You crying with me? Mark's Yours. Help me to remember that. My denial about the crisis is fading, but now I must guard and control my thoughts. Lord, help me find the praiseworthy things.

My continual prayer: "There's healing for Mark in the name of Jesus. At His command, at the touch of His hand, there's healing for Mark in the name of Jesus."

◆   ◆   ◆

Mark was still on two antibiotics for the tracheal infection and now three medications for the high blood pressure. He was weaker and had lost 28 pounds. I completed the range-of-motion exercises with Mark's arms, hands, feet, and legs. Like a wooden soldier, his joints had to be pushed back and forth.

MONDAY, AUGUST 29

I'm not getting the exercise I need even though I walk up to the fourth floor and also take the stairs when leaving. How embarrassing! I locked myself out of the car again. AAA rescued me.

I'm sure getting my money's worth.

I think I'm stuck in a whirlpool, out of the main current.

Lord, don't let me lose my grip.

TUESDAY, AUGUST 30

I'm struggling with a phone call I received from someone who was trying to help.

She said, "It seems that such a horrible accident could only happen to a bad person."

I sat stunned and speechless.

She continued, "Have you accepted your circumstances? What is your attitude toward God? Do you have resentment? God doesn't always heal, you know."

Her last comment hit me the hardest, but I couldn't tell her how well I knew.

Finally I was able to say, "I claim victory for each breath I take." For some reason these words quieted her. And I knew I couldn't take offense at her queries, remembering Christ's command to forgive seventy times seven.

My frayed emotions are allowing my friend's questioning to possess me. She seems to be equating tragedy with transgression. I don't need more guilt and blame. I need reassurance and consolation. If agony produces growth, I'm flourishing.

Yet, I soon think of those who don't say much, but their actions let us know they care. They think they have no answers, but God's language speaks through them. Just walking beside us, they lessen our pain.

I've come to believe that when the shock of grief is the freshest, words should be the fewest. I must practice trusting God more so I can have some peace.

◆ ◆ ◆

Mark continued on medications for his infection and high blood pressure and showed improving trends. When the therapists strapped him to a slant board and gradually raised him toward a vertical position for the first time, they were pleased to see that his blood pressure did not soar as it might have. Mark looked distraught, but I was thrilled because it meant he had some feeling.

WEDNESDAY, AUGUST 31

God loves us daily through others, and that's a force that inspires me to be faithful. One friend wrote: "No one could doubt your love for Him and your confidence in Him! It's really blessed me to be your friend at such a time."

She sees something in me that came only from You, Lord. Thank You for that.

◆ ◆ ◆

The social worker, Shelia Cronin, was a brisk, matter-of-fact person. When I went into her office for our prearranged appointment, she introduced herself by bluntly saying, "My objective is to help your family cope with a severely brain-damaged son."

She may have been trying to be kind, but her words emotionally shattered me when she expressed little hope for Mark's progress.

"Do you realize the seriousness of Mark's head injury?" she asked.

"Yes, I do."

Deaf to my answer she persisted, "The sooner you face reality, the less conflict you'll have. Your adjustment will be healthier, too. You should step back and redirect your energies."

I interrupted, suddenly re-energized to say, "But that's not an option! I feel confident that God will choose to heal Mark. I refuse to accept the medical statistics. Mark, I believe, will be a medical exception," and went on to say, "I have seen times when God overruled human logic."

"I've never met anyone with the depth of your conviction," she said, closing with a sigh. She left the session open-ended so I would feel free to return. Had I planted a seed?

THURSDAY, SEPTEMBER 1

Will the social worker figure out how to include God in future contacts with confused families? Though drained, I'm still hopeful.

Bob, by choice, isn't here to give me support. He went to the coast for an extended, 4-day weekend saying he was exhausted. He wanted me to go, too, but I couldn't leave Mark. Was I crazy to think Mark needed us?

I proposed that we stay in town and alternate two-day visiting responsibilities. "Bob, what if Mark worsened and we were out of town?"

"Don't fall prey to your usual persistent, pessimistic perceptions," he intoned.

"Bob, don't leave me," I pleaded.

However, he ignored me and departed while I seethed. Could I forgive him? Did he think he was the only one who was exhausted? How could he abandon Kathy and me?

Even jotting this down makes me feel better. I know Bob is in pain, too. Is he admitting his limitations while I'm ignoring mine? Anyway, we're not communicating well.

◆   ◆   ◆

Five nurses rallied around Mark and transferred him from the bed into a wheelchair. With pillows and a waist belt, they propped him up for six minutes, continually monitoring his blood pressure. The nurses considered the first sit-up successful, but Mark seemed troubled. Between his feeding tube and the "trach" tube, which supplied air, he was struggling to breathe. Panic registered in his eyes.

Anne visited Mark frequently and I always received a side benefit-affectionate hugs. I wondered how long she could handle the stress. "Anne, we don't want you feeling obligated. If you need to walk away from our trauma, we'll understand," I said.

"You're selling me short," she replied as her eyes narrowed and cheeks flushed. I was taken back by her retort yet, at the same time, felt I had underestimated her.

FRIDAY, SEPTEMBER 2

Anne does a superb job of providing audible stimulation for Mark by reading to him. Often when we come to see Mark she is there. Although Mark makes no response, she talks to him, telling him when she'll stop by again.

None of us know how long and painful Mark's journey will be. Will she be able to endure? I hope so.

◆   ◆   ◆

That day I asked Anne what qualities she most admired in Mark.

"Well, as a teacher he cares about those who hurt. He helps those who find difficulty adjusting or feeling comfortable in social settings." She hesitated, smiled, and added, "He's thoughtful and a gentleman. He opens the car door for me, and I'm not used to that. But I assure you, I like it."

Bob called and wanted another progress report. I was weary and still unhappy that he left town and found it difficult to be civil. Finally, I told him that if he wanted a detailed update he should call the hospital.

FRIDAY, SEPTEMBER 2 (Cont.)

Lord, I must admit that I feel guilty about my response to Bob. Please help me deal with my anger. Give us Your wisdom in this conflict. I long to be free of guilt and show my obedience to You.

SATURDAY, SEPTEMBER 3

When Kathy and I reviewed several tests with the medical team, we were delighted to learn that Mark's sinuses were normal. The CT scan revealed no swelling, bleeding, excess liquid, or infection in the brain. Still, the damaged (low density) area on the left side of the brain remained the same.

Dr. Markham said, "Mark shows signs of being rehabilitatable. The coma is lessening, but the process will be slow. Don't expect too much."

What a thrill to know Mark will wake up. But will he talk? Will he walk? Will he be able to dress and feed himself? No one but You, God, has these answers. Yet, I believe that Mark will be restored.

Coping with the painful uncertainties, however, grows more difficult. The agony of watching Mark paralyzes me and I struggle, too, because Kathy's faith is being assaulted.

"My concept of God has changed," she confessed. "I even wonder if there is a God."

That blow devastated me!

Like the man who said to you, Jesus, "I believe, help Thou my unbelief," don't let me lose hope. I look forward to tomorrow's worship service. Meanwhile, help me image You.

7

Prayer Power

○ ○

Prayer serves as an edge and border to preserve the web of life.

—Robert Hall

In the pulpit Sunday morning Pastor said, "Before we pray, I want to talk about Mark Laughlin. He's been in a coma since August 11.

"Just before his accident Mark had entered seminary in preparation for missions. The college students have rallied around Mark spiritually and contributed to round-the-clock prayer. Every time I go into his room someone is here ministering to him.

"As I talk to many of his own age, I see the bewildered look in their eyes…For those of you who ask, 'Why?' I have to say, 'I don't really know. God allowed it.' I do know that His sovereign wisdom had something in mind that my finite wisdom can't comprehend'…

"Let's pray for Mark continually'…

"Loving Father, we acknowledge that You are God. In the midst of all the imponderables of life, we acknowledge again that we love You and trust You…We ask in behalf of Mark…that he might be healed."

SUNDAY, SEPTEMBER 4

Pastor's words are always an inspiration to my soul. I'm thankful that every Sunday Mark's remembered in prayer. Yet if Mark dies will I think that his death is Your doing, Lord? That You wanted Mark to die or that You are in control and gave Your consent to his death?

Ruth Ann Tidswell said, "Our church needs to see a miracle. Kathy needs to see that miracle, too. She needs to know that there's a dimension beyond medical science that's totally outside her control."

This comment, coming from my best friend, cheered my heart, Lord. I could see You working through her.

◆   ◆   ◆

When Bob returned from the beach my anger had lessened. I resolved I'd not bring the issue up.

Then we were told that hospital chaplain Novak recently spoke to a group of Catholic chaplains. "Initially no one but Mark's parents felt their son would live. But every time I go by Mark's room I observe someone ministering and praying…I've complete faith that young man will get well."

SUNDAY, SEPTEMBER 4 (Cont.)

Lord, where do faith and hope meet the boundaries of reality? Give me rest within my troubled heart. Will August 11th be one of my happiest, yet one of my saddest, memories? Will you choose to heal Mark? Can we accept a different son if he is less than what Mark was? Will Mark be able to accept who he is? Lord, I am confused, yet You are sovereign. Help us accept Your will for Mark.

◆   ◆   ◆

The hospital staff counseled us. They also provided printed materials regarding head trauma patients' levels of awareness. As Mark's coma lessened he:

- likely would have a limited ability to process information. Possible bizarre behavior could include fear and anxiety;

- might over-respond to stimulus even after its removal;

- might remove tubes, crawl out of bed, or be hostile;

- would not be able to talk until the tracheal tube was replaced by a plug. With his finger over the plug, Mark likely would learn to vocalize although his speech could be confused or inappropriate to the setting. If lacking memory, he might invent details;

- might lack social judgment and former hygiene standards;

- might have problems with learning and recall, and be unable to reason;

- might have loss of emotional control or be depressed; and

- might have impairment of hearing, sight, taste, smell, or feelings.

◆   ◆   ◆

Mark's injury could also cause other symptoms similar to those of a stroke victim's. These were speech and language problems including the language disorder called aphasia: the ability to think of a word or concept, but the inability to speak or write thoughts. He could also have anomia: the inability to remember proper names.

MONDAY, SEPTEMBER 5

The information, though mind-boggling, gives us guidelines as Mark progresses. To realize that his responses fit within the norm for a head-trauma patient is reassuring and provides a coma recovery yardstick.

What terrifies me is that Mark might not be able to write or verbally express his thoughts. I know, Lord, that you haven't authored the spirit of fear that possesses me. Being emotionally exhausted, I wrestled with the uncertainties.

In spite of all this, Mark shows improvement. His left eye can open wide. Thank You, God, Kathy's fear that his left eye nerves might be permanently damaged is not true. Another great victory.

◆   ◆   ◆

Daily Mark sat up for approximately one-half hour at noon and evening if his blood pressure didn't soar too high. Three staff persons lifted Mark from the bed into the braked wheelchair. Although cushioned in a pillow, his head lolled and fell backward. He couldn't hold his body upright and his mouth gaped so that he drooled on his gown and had difficulty swallowing. He looked bewildered. His arms and legs hung motionless.

As Bob wheeled Mark down the hallway, I kept him upright by holding his head erect, wiped away his drools, and watched that his feet didn't slide off the footrests. He actually looked out the hall window and saw the lights of the city. For a moment he seemed captivated, but his eyes soon closed and then his head pressed heavily against my hands. This short flicker of awareness, however, excited Bob and me.

What hurt most was that people stared at Mark. Didn't they realize how rude their prolonged curiosity seemed? Although Bob said nothing, I sensed their actions pained him, too.

TUESDAY, SEPTEMBER 6

How I appreciated Dr. Robert Driessen, the lung specialist who supervised Mark's respiratory treatments. His tender concern showed in all his actions.

Dr. Driessen noticed that Mark seemed more agitated than usual sitting in his chair this evening. Noting our son's discomfort, the doctor told the nurse, "Put Mark back to bed immediately."

"Mark is fortunate to have such a supportive family," he told Bob and me. It was so encouraging to see such sensitivity in a doctor. Every conversation we shared with him left us feeling loved and looking forward to our next contact. With his supervision, Mark's tracheal infection had shown gradual improvement.

At first the nurses didn't monitor Mark's blood pressure as closely as I thought they should. When he was set up it would rise; when he was laid back down it would stabilize. When Mark was put to bed today his stress continued so I sat by his bed, holding his hand, and for an hour murmured prayers for him.

Gradually Mark quieted. Later, when the nurse on duty commented that he appeared more restful, she rechecked and told me she had found a significant drop in Mark's blood pressure. Our eyes met and we smiled. Thank You, Lord.

Nightly I looked forward to my angel nurse. She was like a gentle touch from Your hand, Lord. No mere words could express my love and appreciation for her. She also gave Mark back rubs and spoke to him in a sensitive manner.

"My three children pray for Mark five times a day," angel said. "When a prayer time slips by, one of my girls reminds me, 'We must pray for Mark, NOW.' We've taped a picture of Mark on our fridge for a prayer reminder," she added.

I gave her the usual goodnight bear hug.

◆   ◆   ◆

After work, since Mark's eyes were focusing more consistently, I brought a mirror and showed him his beard. I'd posted a large-numbered calendar and encouraged him to focus on the date and then marked off the day. I also hung a large-faced clock and pointed to its hands and watched, with joy, as Mark focused on the numbers.

Anne stayed with Mark while Kathy and I reluctantly went shopping. Life outside the hospital room went on. In this case I was determined to help Kathy find a suit to wear when interviewing for her all-important three-year residency. Emotionally, neither of us wanted to leave Mark for a minute. At first she persisted in her decision to cancel her countrywide residency interview trip. But Bob and I finally convinced her to go, telling her Mark would want her to fulfill her commitment.

WEDNESDAY, SEPTEMBER 7

The throngs of happy people chattered and laughed, oblivious to our tragedy, while Kathy and I walked like robots. How we found a suit I'll never know.

What a parched desert. I've never felt so alone and forsaken. Where are You, God? The sole fact that sustains my sanity is that You know and, with love, have given Your consent. But I still don't understand.

We dashed back to the hospital and rushed up four flights of stairs to be with Mark. As we walked into the room Anne looked up, her eyes shining. "He placed his left hand on mine," she said.

THURSDAY, SEPTEMBER 8

For the first time, Mark moved his hand! I was so excited. We women hugged each other and thanked You, Lord.

Speaking of thanks, here's another one for the excellent staff that cares for Mark. I especially appreciate nurse Shirley Berglund who has a rare touch. To her Mark is an intelligent man, not an object. She speaks softly and reassuringly. She lovingly asks Mark's permission or tells him what she is doing and why. When completed, she reinforces the learning by telling him what she did. She expresses her loving care in everything she does, displaying the qualities of an ideal nurse enjoying her profession. I really love her, Lord.

◆   ◆   ◆

We were ready for more good news and got it. Mark's blood pressure was lower. The tracheal infection had lessened. The therapists reported that they were pleased with Mark's progress on the slant board. Gradually the board was used to lift him to a vertical position helping to stabilize his blood pressure. Mark also had some movement in his arms.

Bob sent progress reports to 75 out-of-state prayer partners, clinging to hope, in spite of his fears. In response to one of his letters the president of WCBS wrote: "We remember Mark in our daily prayers…a full tuition refund is enclosed…It is our prayer that Mark may be restored to full health and be able to return to seminary."

FRIDAY, SEPTEMBER 9

A verse shared by friends became words to live by as I quoted it to Mark: "'For I know the plans I have for you,' declares the Lord, 'plans to prosper you and not to harm you, plans to give you hope and a future'" (Jer. 29:11).

Bob and I have meditated on this text daily. We have prayed, Lord, that Your healing will be Mark's experience. We want to lean fully on You, remaining full of hope. Do I see a light at the end of the tunnel or is it an oncoming train? That's a negative thought, Lord, but we've had one shock after another. I guess I'm just trying to protect myself.

SATURDAY, SEPTEMBER 10

What I've just experienced has torn me apart, Lord, but more importantly, I'm wondering if Mark is also going through emotional pain. He lies helpless in bed-diapered, invaded by tracheal, feeding, and catheter tubes. What is his level of awareness? Did he hear what I heard as I came into his room this morning?

The curtain around Mark's bed was drawn so, although I couldn't see them, I could hear the nurse. Apparently she had turned Mark on his side, removed his full diaper, and dropped it to the floor. To my shock, I then heard two swats on flesh as she admonished him as though he were a threeyear-old. "Shame on you, Mark." Further shock-I heard several steps-and she shrieked again, "Shame, shame. Looks just like chocolate and I've stepped in the mess."

Appalled, my maternal instinct rose within me like a warhorse to the sound of battle. Barely constraining myself, I walked around the drawn curtain to confront her, "Don't talk to my son in such a demeaning manner."

"I'm sorry. I meant no offense." Flushed, she said, "But I understand what you are saying." I forced a smile.

The issue is closed but I must admit, Lord, it still bothers me. Is Mark bothered, too? God, please blot this experience from our minds.

◆   ◆   ◆

A speech pathologist tested Mark during the mid-morning. To avoid distracting Mark I listened while sitting on the hall floor outside his room. As the specialist asked questions he instructed Mark to look at either a large "Yes" or "No" card. The pathologist complimented Mark as he gave responses that revealed orientation to person, place, position, age, and sex.

The specialist continued testing by asking Mark to respond by opening or closing his mouth or eyes, or looking at objects. Mark responded with answers to only three of the nine requests, all correct, and the pathologist and I felt encouraged.

As we shook hands the specialist said, "I'll pray for Mark," and left.

SATURDAY, SEPTEMBER 10 (Cont.)

I'll have to admit the results of the tests and the pathologist's promise lifted my troubled heart.

I had a pleasant afternoon bedside visit with Mark. Most of the time he appeared restful and his eyes remained closed. During these intervals, as deaconess chairperson, I planned my agenda for our next meeting. It doesn't seem possible that a month has passed since the last meeting on August 14. Numbness carried me through that session.

Pastor lovingly has encouraged me to resign my deaconess position if I became too pressured. Lord, as you know, I've resigned all other church responsibilities but believe I need the close fellowship of this supportive group. Tomorrow I will quote 2 Timothy 1:7: "For God did not give us a spirit of timidity, but a spirit of power, of love and of self-discipline."

I will ask them as a group to claim this victorious truth. Lord, I believe you will provide the extra strength I need.

During mid-afternoon Mark appeared somewhat alert and his eyes focused. Since Mark's coma, I had daily worn a small, three-belled necklace that he had given me. As I spoke of, and pointed to, the chain Mark glanced at the strands of gold. To check his awareness and responsiveness, I put my hand several inches above Mark's and asked him to raise his left hand up to mine. With an upward, faltering motion he touched my hand.

Lord, only You know how overjoyed I was! He actually heard me. His brain processed the message. He voluntarily acted upon the request. I hugged him. "I'm so excited, Mark. You are doing great." I beamed.

He showed no emotions. Oh, God, please may his emotional center not be destroyed. Kathy had alluded to that possibility, but I couldn't accept that.

I then showed Mark a booklet of twenty-three pictorial letters with short notes saying, "We are praying and hoping you will get well so you can wake up." This booklet came from a third grade class in a San Francisco Bay area Christian school whose teacher was Mark's friend. Mark still remained unresponsive.

◆   ◆   ◆

On our way to church Bob told me, "While driving to Men's Round-Up at Camp Tadmor yesterday, I remembered the many times Mark and I traveled there and couldn't stop crying." He hesitated and swallowed hard before continuing.

"Larry McCracken, the Director of Conservative Baptist Association (CBA) of Oregon asked about Mark. He planned to speak about and pray for him, but asked me to make a report to the group. My comments and McCracken's sensitive remarks must have touched hearts. The director asked that the 1,500 men stand and clasp hands while he prayed. A swell of electrifying and awesome emotion swept throughout the hall."

SUNDAY, SEPTEMBER 11

A most encouraging moment occurred after the morning church service, one month after Mark's surgeries. When Bob and I walked onto the 4th floor corridor, Mark's nurse rushed toward us beaming with excitement. She redeemed her yesterday's behavior by saying, "Mark fisted and opened both his hands!" Thank You, Lord.

This afternoon the 23-member deaconess committee showered me with affirmation and promised their continued prayers. I left that meeting, my soul afloat. Thanks Lord for hugging me through these beautiful, caring women.

◆   ◆   ◆

During the evening several of Mark's former high school students and a student's mother visited Mark again. One of the students said, "We didn't consider Mark just our teacher; he was our best friend, too."

The mother said to the group, "I've appreciated Mark's handling of my son." In her quiet way, she added, "If it hadn't been for Mark's recommendation he would have been expelled. No one would give him another chance. I remember Mark daily in my prayers." She suggested we pray for Mark and we did. They bid us farewell and departed.

I hugged Mark goodnight. Before leaving I meditated on another uniquely designed poster brought by a caring family.

I also thought of our retired dentist, Dr. Walter Johnson, who says he often walks to the hospital, roves the halls to sense the atmosphere surrounding Mark and then prays.

8

A Priceless Gift

○ ○

Love is not only something you feel. It's something you do.

—David Wilkerson

For the first time, Mark squeezed my hands. "Great job, Mark." I beamed. I noticed that his left hand grip was stronger than the right hand grip, but this was great progress.

The flow of visitors continued unabated, and letters poured in. Recently one came from a lovely woman who was Mark's first date. Though married, she had written him saying, "Some relationships seem to sustain themselves on fond memories. You still have a special place in my heart and always will."

During the evening she visited Mark. As she sat down she placed her hand on his arm.

"Remember me? I'm Cindy from Adams High School."

I believe Mark recognized Cindy but soon he drifted off as if asleep. She took it well, and sat with him for a moment as she and I talked, but left when other visitors arrived.

MONDAY, SEPTEMBER 12

I rushed home to read our daily mail that always nourished me. A Sunday school student from 25 years ago wrote, "Ever since you taught me in junior high, Milli, I have regarded you as someone special. In this situation you are indeed proving that!"

Thank You, Lord, for this note and all the other kind people who send cards. They validate Your constant love and bring us comfort.

◆   ◆   ◆

Bob stopped by to see Mark and then left on a four-day business trip. But encouraging cards, letters, telegrams, and calls continued to flow in like a tide of love. One letter stated, "How we pray for God's complete healing for Mark...God gave me a vision of Mark on Sunday morning, September 11. There was a brilliant rainbow over his head. It was about 9:00 a.m. your time...I'd like to know what was happening on that day and at that time."

I quickly wrote a note to this inquirer telling him that Mark was a budding miracle. In the note I said, "Near 9:00 a.m. our time he fisted and opened his hands."

TUESDAY, SEPTEMBER 13

Lord, I can't tell you what a thrill Mark's fisting and our friend's faith gave to me.

But taking Mark for his evening stroll was difficult without Bob's assistance. Mark showed a mixture of little awareness and puzzlement. Lord, was it also because Bob was not here? Mark needs us and I need Bob.

WEDNESDAY, SEPTEMBER 14

This evening Dr. Markham stopped by to test Mark's tracking. For once, when the doctor was present, Mark "performed" well. On command he looked at the kite and his eyes focused on the clock and calendar. Elated, Dr. Markham demanded of us, "Aren't you excited?"

"We expect great things," I said, beaming.

Anne was visiting Mark, too. We both experienced a real upward mood swing when we saw Mark's responses. However, we knew we lived on an emotional roller coaster.

◆   ◆   ◆

Kathy had applied the previous spring for a Mission Assistance Program from Reader's Digest International Fellowship. One winner of this honor was chosen from each state. In mid-September they notified her that she was one of the fifty recipients.

Kathy had received unanimous approval from Hinson's mission committee for a short-term assignment at the Lorimar Hospital in Rwanguba, Zaire the coming spring.

"But I don't want to leave Mark," Kathy exclaimed. She made this statement even though she had looked forward to a medical mission since she was six years old.

"You must go, Kathy," I exhorted. "We support God's leading in your life."

WEDNESDAY, SEPTEMBER 14 (Cont.)

How can I be so happy for Kathy and yet have no certainty of Mark's progress? A sobering emotional paradox. But, Lord, you are sovereign. I pray I'll be able to walk into the unknown, trusting You.

◆   ◆   ◆

Bob and I had an appointment with the director of Providence's rehab center Friday. Because Bob was out of town, again, I met alone with the director, Mr. Miller, who was accompanied by our social worker. Neither were optimists. Although I realized they had to avoid giving false hopes, the one-hour session was disheartening.

"Mark's physical and medical care has moved from acute and unstable to chronic and predictable," the director said. "Assuming Mark has no reversals, you can soon look at some options. Mark can remain at 4R18 and we'll double his therapy. He can move to our rehabilitation unit. He can transfer to another rehab center in the area." Miller paused and looked at me before continuing, "Or, he can transfer to a chronic care institution."

To this point I had listened, nodding my head. Now I protested, "He'll never go to a nursing home. Never!"

I flashed back to thoughts of my beloved mother who lay bedfast, without complaint, for 19 years. Her gnarled, withered 68-pound body was little more than bones and bedsores when she died.

I can't watch Mark waste away, too. It's too hard to bear. Oh, God, please spare Mark that torture.

Hurriedly, the director replied, "Of course, of course. I understand."

He explained their plan for promoting Mark's independence and mobility. "His progress will be slow. You shouldn't set your expectations too high. Mark could plateau at any moment."

Shaken, I replied, "I'll review these options with Bob and Kathy. Then we'll give you our decision."

THURSDAY, SEPTEMBER 15

Today I toured 3L, the rehab unit with the director. Located in an older part of the hospital, the small rooms were drab, but clean. The setting did not foster optimism, Lord. Most of the patients were elderly individuals who had had strokes or broken bones. How would Mark fit in?

However, several Christian nurses introduced themselves when they knew Mark might be moved to their unit.

The head nurse, a sturdy, cheerful person, bustled up to me and said, "Your son sang a solo at my daughter's wedding. What a fine tenor voice he has. We look forward to caring and praying for Mark."

I grabbed and hugged her. "Thank you for your kind words," I said in a choked voice. "Your focus is on target. I'm thrilled you'll pray for Mark."

Lord, should this rehab unit be Mark's next move? Help me think about the words of the nurses rather than the comments of the director.

◆   ◆   ◆

That evening when I walked into Mark's room I was shocked to see blood around his neck incision, on his gown, the bedspread, cards, walls, ceiling-everywhere. They had changed Mark's trach again. The procedure should have been simple and relatively painless, shouldn't it? Why hadn't they cleaned up this mess?

To get rid of this sight I washed Mark's neck and sponged his gown. With soap, water, and a washcloth, I cleaned everything within reach. Only a portion of the ceiling, directly over Mark's bed, was unreachable. When the job was done I was too weary to confront nurses. Furthermore, I had to rush to the airport to pick up Bob.

At that low point in my life, my dear Anne walked in, hugged me, and comforted me. What a fantastic supporter. I left Mark in her care while I drove to the airport.

FRIDAY, SEPTEMBER 16

Lord, I'm grateful Bob is home. We all need each other. Also, thanks for another hug from You, Lord; a business man often prays while eating his lunch at Mark's bedside.

◆   ◆   ◆

When we explored the options for Mark's future care, Kathy recommended the Rehabilitation Institute of Oregon (RIO). She said the facility was one of the finest. How providential for us that Kathy knew of this source.

Because Mark was a brain-injured patient, his medical insurance allowed sixty days of in-house therapy instead of thirty. This relieved some anxiety.

Kathy and I faced the possible costs beyond medical coverage. The lung therapy alone had now cost over $9,000.00.

"Expenses will never be a factor," Kathy said. "My brother will receive the best care possible. I'll work the rest of my life to pay for it."

"Oh, Kathy," I responded, "You know Bob and I will, too."

SATURDAY, SEPTEMBER 17

Lord, this accident has allowed our family to be more open and honest with each other as we work to help Mark.

Even the CBA of Oregon Family News is featuring a monthly progress report on Mark. Also, Diana Smith, liaison for JBC, is keeping the student body current regarding Mark's progress.

Lord, thank You for countless prayer warriors.

◆   ◆   ◆

Bob, Kathy, and I went to our RIO appointment that included a tour of the complex. Our assigned social worker, Susan Swanson, was confident Mark could be helped. What a change of atmosphere. The facility and her bright attitude generated hope. We sensed they had much to offer Mark. I was so moved I hugged her before we left.

Mark's next transfer, we decided, would involve a move to the Providence Rehab Unit when he was alert enough. Later he would transfer to RIO.

SATURDAY, SEPTEMBER 17 (Cont.)

When I visited Mark this afternoon he frowned. Thank You, Lord, his center of emotions has not been destroyed. But why did he keep frowning? Neither Anne nor I could do anything during the afternoon to erase his frown. Then in walked that model nurse, Shirley, to save the day.

She checked her patient before turning to us and gracefully asking us to step out in the hall, as she drew the curtain around Mark's bed. When we were invited back in we were struck by how peaceful Mark appeared. An ordinary event, having a bowel movement, was extraordinary for Mark. How thrilling that, for the first time since his accident, Mark had feeling in his lower torso.

Yes, Lord, this has been a very good day.

◆   ◆   ◆

In the morning service, Pastor spoke on Ezekiel and again prayed for Mark. His message was printed in outline form in the bulletin.

"The Pastor's message is perfect for Mark," said Annette Jumonville, a teacher friend. "Would you mind if one of the art instructors printed the five points so we can hang the poster in Mark's room?"

"That's a great idea," I responded. "When Bob, Kathy, and I go to the hospital today, I'll tell them about your plan." Kathy and I had planned a remembrance of Bob's birthday, hoping it would jog Mark's memory. Kathy sat by her brother's bedside, taking his hand. "Mark, this is September 18th, Dad's birthday. I have a gift for him from both you and me. When you can help plan the event, we'll celebrate more."

Mark remained listless and unresponsive. Bob unwrapped his birthday gift anyway. "I'll read my cards later. But, Mark, I'm glad we could remember my birthday as a family."

We felt let down by Mark's lack of response. He always had been a great planner for special days. Could we hope he would have this creative talent again?

SUNDAY, SEPTEMBER 18

Lord, thank you for the exciting news this evening that has cheered us after today's disappointment.

The head nurse told us, "Mark has advanced to a level of awareness beyond the coma (after 39 days). We plan to transfer him to the Rehab Unit (3L) tomorrow. His therapy will be increased."

What a happy ending you gave us to Bob's birthday. Only You, Lord, could have given him-and us-such a priceless gift.

9

First Written Words

Hope is one of the principal springs that keeps mankind in motion.

—Andrew Fuller

The rehab director greeted us when we arrived with Mark on 3L15 the morning of the 19th. He suggested, since the room was small, that we take Mark's paraphernalia home. Mark frowned and looked angry. We quickly compromised. Many of his gifts, cards, posters, and plants went home with us, but one item was an exception.

In speech therapy Mark had been taught to nod his head "Yes" or "No." When I asked Mark if I could take the kite home he frowned. With slight movement of his head, I knew the answer. Immediately I decided Mark's artistic creation would hang from the ceiling.

MONDAY, SEPTEMBER 19

Lord, we are glad that Mark's rehab room is across from the nurses' station, another affirmation of Your love for us.

As I left for work, the head nurse said, "Every person in 3L15 gets well." We shared a smile.

Lord, how I appreciated her cordial manner and optimism. She is the first person at the hospital to project hope.

Mark's move, from one unit to another, proved upsetting. He frowned and remained tense and distressed. All except one of his nurses and therapists were new. These changes compounded the trauma in his small, muddled world.

As previously planned, Annette Jumonville visited Mark and hung a large poster for his easy viewing:

A LESSON FROM EZEKIEL

GOD KNOWS WHERE YOU ARE AND WHY
GOD STILL LOVES YOU.
GOD HAS PLANS FOR YOU.
GOD KNOWS HOW TO TAKE CARE OF
   YOUR ENEMIES.
GOD STILL PLANS A MAGNIFICENT
   FUTURE FOR YOU.

Lord, I believe these words. But seeing Mark helpless hurts my heart and shakes my faith. I find the pain ceaseless. When will relief come?

WEDNESDAY, SEPTEMBER 21

Mark was calmer this morning. He looks forward to the early visit from Bob. Playing the role of the incurable optimist, Bob strengthens Mark's spirits. I feel my husband's morning visit is like an anchor for Mark.

"Son, I've never been prouder of you," Bob states daily. I add, "Mark, with God you can do it."

Mark seems to be taking pride in his gains.

◆   ◆   ◆

Mark had "organic emotional lability," a loss of emotional control due to his brain injury. When the nurses readied him for his strolls we could tell by the sparkle in his eyes how much he anticipated the treat, but despair followed. As he quickly tired, he seemed to sense his hopelessness. Again his expectations dissolved into a prolonged, tearful wheelchair journey.

"We're glad you can express yourself," I said. "Your tears don't embarrass us." Sometimes diverting his attention helped him regain self-control.

Mark still lacked balance. While sitting up and attempting to swallow, he would gasp and gurgle, episodes that terrified all of us. He, therefore, wanted to lie down long before the scheduled time. But these spells were lessening. However, his head continued to tilt backward. His mouth gaped, and he had no leg movement. Yet, when Bob coaxed him that evening, Mark waved good-bye to us with a flailing motion of his left hand.

Meanwhile, the speech therapist had taught Mark how to smile again in spite of the paralysis on the right side of his face. Mark hadn't completely mastered the task yet.

Six weeks after the accident Mark had learned to type on an alphabetical keyboard that printed out onto a tape. We received an ecstatic written report from the speech therapist although her professional manner demanded an understatement of extraordinary progress. "Patient making improvements in communication skills. He demonstrates improved ability to use Canon Communicator. He was oriented to person, place, date, age, and date of birth. He typed a few sentences. He made a verbal sound. He typed: 'Dumb. That's not talking.'"

Was the Mark we loved coming back to us?

THURSDAY, SEPTEMBER 22

I'm grateful that Mark is left-handed because of the paralysis on his right side. His left arm continues to strengthen. Yet, Mark misspells words, or writes sentences making no sense. Often he can't reach the top row of letters because of the immobility in his left arm.

Today Mark became frustrated when I couldn't understand what he'd typed. After several attempts, discouraged, he refused to use the communicator.

The therapists have told us we must encourage Mark's use of the instrument. Here, my instincts balked to see him so tormented. I often reverted to finding his needs by trial and error or having him nod or shake his head.

He was at our mercy, Lord, and we had to be merciful.

FRIDAY, SEPTEMBER 23

I, again, made several attempts to read Mark's typed communications but couldn't understand anything.

Shredded by fear that Mark may suffer from deep aphasia, I appeal to You, oh God. His mind seems to be unhinged. In shock, I wait, terrified. The fear that floods my soul overwhelms me. It seems too heavy to bear.

◆   ◆   ◆

My journalizing was interrupted by the shrill ringing of the phone. It was Kathy saying, in a shaky voice, "I took Mark for a stroll this afternoon."

I knew immediately that something awful had happened.

She went on, "I pushed him in his chair through the door in front of the full-length mirrors. For the first time he saw his gaunt and helpless frame and shaven head. He was slumped in his wheelchair-masked in strange and protruding tubes. When Mark realized he was looking at himself, he lifted his head and cried aloud. Mom, I wept, too."

I was at a loss for words.

Kathy took a deep breath and continued. "We returned to Mark's room and the nurse put him back in bed. I asked Mark if he wanted the communicator and he nodded. But nothing he typed made any sense. Propped on his pillow he just lay there in despair. I couldn't help him. I was distraught and drained and had to leave. Everything looked bleak and hopeless."

What could I say?

"On my way out," Kathy went on, "I rushed into a first floor restroom. I was crying again. I clenched my fists. I beat on the walls until my knuckles were numb. I hated God. I even thought of killing you, Mark, Dad, and myself. How else could I relieve this endless misery?

"Guilt flooded over me. How could I have such evil thoughts? Mom, aren't I awful?" "Of course not, sweetheart—we're all in such pain. You had to have some release."

FRIDAY, SEPTEMBER 23 (Cont.)

Kathy and I know that we will never again take Mark through the hall with full-length mirrors. Why hadn't someone warned us? My heart aches for Kathy.

When she lashed out at You, my life-line and only hope, I wondered, what next? Where else could I turn? Who else could help if I, too, lost faith in You?

SATURDAY, SEPTEMBER 24

This morning I woke up in hell, that deep black pit that I knew all too well. The diagnosis: depression. I vividly remembered the unrelenting mental pain, excruciating and intolerable depths of despair accompanied by a death wish. Twenty years ago I suffered depression caused by a thyroid/endocrine imbalance after removal of a malignant thyroid gland. Now depression possesses me again.

Oh, God, can I bear this, too?

◆   ◆   ◆

Forcing myself out of bed, I dressed, ate a bite, and drove to the hospital. Within minutes Kathy arrived. When she saw me her doctor-instinct knew I needed help.

"Kathy, I just want to die," I said, void of tears. "I'm so depressed."

"Mom, depression doesn't usually occur so quickly. But it's not surprising since you've been under constant strain. We need to consult with the hospital pharmacist immediately."

They gave me a two-day prescription of the smallest dosage of a non-habit forming antidepressant. I'd taken this before, during my endocrine imbalance. They told me to see my doctor on Monday.

SATURDAY, SEPTEMBER 24 (Cont.)

In the afternoon Mark actually reached out and took the hand of another visitor, Cary, a young, alcoholic friend whom he had counseled.

"Mark," Cary said softly, "it's great to see you."

Mark focused his eyes on his visitor. I stepped back and sat down in a corner chair. Cary carried on his conversation with Mark as if I weren't present.

"I don't know God's reason for this. But I thank Him for you. You're in my thoughts and prayers daily."

He hesitated, and then leaned forward.

"There's a gap in our church youth group," he continued. "Please come back and fill that void. You're needed. We miss your sharing and caring. We're not the same without you."

My eyes brimmed with tears. The tightness in my throat made swallowing difficult.

Then, smiling, Cary presented Mark with Odie, a stuffed animal, from the Garfield comic strip. "May he keep you company in my absence." Gripping Mark's hand again, he paused a moment, said "Goodbye," nodded at me, and left.

My heart was thirsty for just such a tender moment.

◆   ◆   ◆

I stayed with Mark during the morning. Over the radio Pastor talked about our son and his severe brain trauma. Mark wept, obviously recognizing Pastor's voice. I had no idea how well he understood what was being said, but was elated to see Mark respond so quickly.

During midweek they had changed the original plastic trach to a metal one and Dr. Driesen said that on the following Wednesday the metal trach would be replaced with a plug. Then Mark, hopefully, could learn to speak.

"Mark has progressed much further than we expected," Dr. Driessen said.

SUNDAY, SEPTEMBER 25

Lord, I appreciate Dr. Driessen's candid, sincere comments and I basked in the medical staff's astonishment at Mark's improvement.

But, why does none of the good news cheer me? A state of well-being and peace of mind eludes me. I can't turn off negative thoughts. My mind spins. Life has changed from a major to a minor key. God, I need Your help as never before.

MONDAY, SEPTEMBER 26

The occupational therapist has said, "Mark's perceptual skills are great." But my emotional fuel gauge is empty. I can't look beyond myself. Climbing stairs exhausts me. Sleep eludes me. Food is flavorless and I have no appetite. I can't concentrate. My thoughts wander. Waves of depression engulf me.

Since I'm in a pit of despondency, Bob and I have agreed that I won't see our son before work or at noon unless Bob travels out of town. I so strongly feel that Mark needs family nearby that I insist I can see Mark when Bob is gone.

For the third time I've locked myself out of the car. My wandering mind can't hold a thought. At least I can have a second car key made.

THURSDAY, SEPTEMBER 29

Lord, what is this roller coaster I'm on? I should be up because of Mark's progress, but for the last two days I've been too shaky inside to write.

◆   ◆   ◆

Pastor must have sensed how Bob and I were struggling because he invited us in for counseling. His easy, loving manner helped us talk about Mark's crisis. What he preached he modeled when he said, "I love you two. How are you really doing?"

I waited for Bob to speak but he sat silent so I said, "This is a painful journey and I'm emotionally drained." I couldn't say the word "depressed" because I was on guard against anyone knowing how I really felt. Twenty years earlier I learned it had been considered unacceptable for a Christian to be depressed. I wasn't about to expose myself again.

"And how's Kathy coping?"

Bob replied bluntly, "Sometimes she's gripped by guilt and bitterness."

Pastor nodded, to let us know he was listening, and then asked, "You've always believed Mark would be healed, haven't you?"

"Yes, we still believe God will restore him," I replied for both of us.

Shaking his head, Pastor declared, "You have preached more sermons in the past 51 days than I have in my ministry. I'm not belittling my ministry, either. I couldn't be more sincere."

Though I tried, I couldn't keep the tears from falling.

Walking over, Pastor put his arms around us and looked intently into our eyes. He prayed, "God, give these dear friends emotional and physical strength. Free Kathy from guilt and bitterness. We ask that Mark's healing might be within Your will."

FRIDAY, SEPTEMBER 30

Only You, Lord, know my deepest thoughts. I battle: guilt, anger, depression. Yet, in spite of all my weaknesses, Pastor said, You can bring good out of this evil. Lord, Your loving, healing touch has reached out again. You planned our meeting with Pastor to encourage and strengthen our weary souls.

◆ ◆ ◆

After lunch at the hospital we were greeted by an excited speech therapist that handed us the speech assignment Mark had written in unsteady, upper case letters:

write your name, write whatever you want   Sept 30

↓MARK HOME←

1. What have you studied?
I HAVE STUDIED BICYCLE MECHANICS.

2. What are your hobbies?
I HAVE TRIPPED TO WASHINGTON D.C..

3. What kind of books do you read?
I'VE NEVER READ A BOOK ON THIS THEME.

I taped the completed assignment on Mark's closet and for a moment moved beyond my depressed self.

When Annette called to invite me out to lunch at a marketplace I was torn. I wanted to tell my dear friend I was deeply depressed but worried about what she would think of me. Besides, having my medication doubled, I'd have to force myself to eat. As a result, I had lost 20 pounds since the accident. How could I eat lunch?

I did go but, because of my dry mouth, had to wash each bite down with a gulp of milk. Afterward, at her suggestion, we toured the complex. I knew she was trying to help, but my thoughts never strayed far from Mark. Colorful shops, the bustle of the crowd, the music-all seemed unreal. All I could think of was, "Why? Why Mark?"

As soon as I politely could, I rushed back to the hospital. Aware of how unstable my mind and emotions had become, I felt I should, instead, be going to a home for the bewildered.

◆   ◆   ◆

During the morning service Pastor said, "This last week I visited Mark Laughlin's room. His room was vacant because he was down at therapy. As I looked around I noticed one poster: 'God is the Blessed Controller of All Things' (1 Tim. 6:15, Phillips). I looked a little further and I saw another inscription, a poster that Annette Jumonville had an art instructor make. This was the five-point outline that I gave you the first Sunday I began preaching from Ezekiel." He continued, "We are learning in our predicaments 'God knows where we are and why.' That's certainly pertinent to Mark. The second point is, 'God still loves us and knows how to perfect us.' That is appropriate to Mark because, even with his limited ability to process so much into his mind right now, Mark may be wondering about God's love.

"Do you know where my eyes settled Wednesday afternoon? Point three: 'God still has a plan for you'...I wonder what sort of message Mark's receiving as he reads these words, 'God still has a plan for you?'...Just the fact this 23 year-old man is showing remarkable progress tells us God's plan for Mark is in process."

That evening, at the end of the service, Pastor asked the Stouts, who had just lost their daughter in a car accident, and us to join him at the front of the church.

"Mom, we still have hope," Kathy whispered. Clasping my hand, she, Bob, and I walked down the aisle to stand in front of the congregation. Pastor walked over to stand with us and said, "These special families are hurting. I'd like the body to unite in prayer. Let's pray for the Stouts in their bereavement and for the Laughlins during Mark's fight to recover.

My eyes puddle as Pastor spoke. Tears dripped from Kathy's chin. We felt love and support from every one of the 400 people there. When the prayer ended I embraced Carol Stout and cried openly for her, Charlie, and us. I hurt for our friends but, at the same time, cherished the fact that we still had hope.

10

Deepest Fears Dispelled

○ ○

The adventurous life is not one exempt from fear, but one that is lived in full knowledge of fears of all kinds, one in which we go forward in spite of our fears.

—Paul Tournier

When Mark whispered "Mom" as Bob and I stepped into 3L15 that evening, we beamed. As thrilled as we were when Mark uttered his first words, nothing ever intoxicated us like this.

The love of others was expressed in many ways. "Mark," I said, "these pictures were drawn by third graders from a San Francisco school. They've made pictures of smiley faces, hills, trees, and sunbeams to show you that they're happy you're awake."

The teacher, a former classmate of Mark's, wrote, "I'm very thankful for the updates your father consistently sends. My kids recognize that, whenever I get a letter from WFECO [Bob's office], it contains news about you. There is always an excited hush. I wish you could have seen them when they heard you were awake. They sent up a cheer that rocked the school."

◆   ◆   ◆

Good news continued. "Mark has spoken his own name," said Carol Saxton, his favorite nurse. "He's said 'Hi" and 'Good morning' to me, too. He's doing fantastically."

The nurses invited me to help Mark with his swallowing. I was shown how to position him upright in bed with neck flexed and chin toward his chest. It was critical that Mark's head not tip back. Because of his poor swallowing reflexes and paralyzed soft palate, Mark had to chew 15 times before swallowing. My job was to ensure his mouth was empty between spoonfuls, then he could repeat the process.

Eating was hard work and Mark perspired heavily. Worse yet, he had to remain upright for half an hour after eating to prevent food backing up from his stomach.

Before leaving late that afternoon, Kathy talked about a paraplegic who had an effective ministry. I knew why she introduced the subject, believing Mark would never walk.

That evening I told Anne what Kathy had said. "Oh, no," she gasped. "I'd never dreamed that Mark wouldn't walk." Paling, she grew silent and pain flared in her eyes. She bit her lip, hesitated, and soon retreated down the hall.

When a nurse told me that movement usually returned to the arms before the legs, I couldn't wait to tell Anne. Reinforcement came quickly when the physical therapist, Margaret O'Rourke, told us, "Mark has strength in his legs. I feel he's going to walk again."

TUESDAY, OCTOBER 4

This has been a great day. Lord, dare I believe that Mark will walk?

◆   ◆   ◆

While making his rounds, Dr. Markham came in to see Mark. "Mark will be ready for RIO soon. He has some feeling in his legs," he said.

When we stepped into the hall, I asked him about Mark's potential to walk.

Dr. Markham hesitated and then declared, "Mark is neurologically imbalanced."

I knew that this meant the doctor believed Mark would never walk. My hopes seemed to crash. But I couldn't give up that quickly. I retorted, "Margaret O'Rourke thinks he'll walk."

Dr. Markham didn't reply. Stunned, I reached for a more hopeful topic. "Well, then tell me when will the urinary catheter be removed?"

He paused, and then replied gently, "Maybe not for weeks. His skin will chap and the clean-up is a messy, time-consuming task."

"I don't understand. Mark has control of his bowels."

Dr. Markham paused and seemed to reconsider. "Oh, I'll check that."

THURSDAY, OCTOBER 6

Great headway, Lord. Dr. Markham removed the catheter.

◆   ◆   ◆

When I visited Mark this evening I read a note on his bed stand. "Mark, I came in to see you, but you were resting so I chose not to wake you. Have a great weekend. I'll be in Salem with my family. Thanks for your gracious written words. You still make me feel beautiful. I'm praying for you. Love, Anne."

FRIDAY, OCTOBER 7

My depression still haunts me and makes me shaky. I still have to make myself eat and can't sleep though the night. In an attempt to comfort myself I've reread some beautiful cards and notes.

- Thanks for that example you give to us; for showing us how Christians meet adversity with grace and dignity. What a lesson.

- I have long admired the Laughlin family, their unswerving faith and loyalty to Christ and the Church. Even now when seeming tragedy has struck I have heard no complaints, but only words of praise and thanks to a wonderful Savior who truly is answering prayers.

People see us-and me, in particular-as strong and able to bear whatever comes. What I know is that I'm at the end of myself. I can't trust my feelings. Oh, God, I feel like a failure.

◆   ◆   ◆

While visiting Mark after our evening church service, Bob, Kathy, and I stood around his bed. He looked at each of us and said, softly, "I love you."

"Mark, with God you can do it. We love you, too," we all replied, chorus-like. Bob and I left with lightened hearts, but Kathy lingered with her brother.

Later she called to tell about the astonishing conversation she and Mark had shared.

"I talked with my brother tonight-I really talked with him. What a privilege! That fearful, black cloud of deep aphasia wasn't true prophecy. I'd like to tell you what he said."

"Yes, I can't wait."

"He asked, 'How was Hinson?'"

"I told Mark about the evening service and the people with whom I'd talked. He cried.

"'Don't cry, Mark,' I said.

"'Okay, I won't, but it would be more honest. It makes people mad when I cry.'"

Kathy said, "I told him, 'Sometimes you start crying and keep going.'

"'I never keep going. Mom gets mad when I act strange,' he told me."

Hearing this from Kathy, I realized I needed to be more careful with my facial expressions. Meanwhile, I asked Kathy, "What did you say?"

"'Nobody's mad at you, Mark.'"

She then told me about the next surprising revelation.

"'I tried to imagine what it would be like my first day back at Western [WCBS], writing about being crippled. It was hard to imagine.'

"'This whole thing has been hard,' I told him. 'It has been anything but glamorous.'

"Then he asked me, 'When will I be able to live at home? How long until I can?'

"I admitted that none of us knew. 'I wish I could say it would be a month, but we need to take it one day at a time. God hasn't told us how long.'

"Dreamily, he said, 'Living at home sounds like...'

"But I couldn't understand his last words.

"Then he said, 'Sometimes I don't feel like talking. I just get fatigued.'

"Mom, I had difficulty understanding most of his labored conversation and asked Mark to repeat words. He spoke softly, one or two words, and then inhaled more air before speaking again. Toward the end Mark grew weary, his words less intelligible. I suggested he rest."

◆   ◆   ◆

SUNDAY, OCTOBER 9

Kathy's talk with Mark dispels our greatest fear. Lord, I thank You that Mark doesn't have deep aphasia, he's writing and speaking-we're overjoyed.

It has been two, long, emotion-packed months since Kathy has shown any enthusiasm, but she was excited now. Bob and I rejoiced in her call and had a hard time falling asleep. Our hopes were fueled again.

TUESDAY, OCTOBER 11

Today it happened. For the first time since the accident Mark stood for a minute with the assistance of two physical therapists. Another great victory.

◆   ◆   ◆

During our next visit Mark told Anne, "My standing is the highlight of the month."

Of course she agreed. He worked hard reaching his goals and, with delight, reported his progress. She inspired Mark by praising him for his determination and accomplishments.

WEDNESDAY, OCTOBER 12

Mark's trach accidentally popped out so Dr. Driessen decided to leave it out, letting the windpipe incision heal. Another bit of progress.

When Kathy talked with Mark about her 21-day residency interview trip she would be taking this coming Friday, they both cried. Mark depended so much on her and she hated to leave him. But between sobs, Mark said, "Do go, Kathy."

FRIDAY, OCTOBER 14

Kathy's departure proved difficult for all of us. Mark said, "You must be tired of my crying."

But the article about his progress in the CBA of Oregon Family News cheered both Mark and me. Thanks for these hugs, too, Lord.

◆   ◆   ◆

Mark had more strength in his right arm. While lying in bed, he flexed his left knee.

Still, he had very short interest and attention spans. He couldn't recall what he'd eaten, heard, or read. Often he couldn't remember visitors' names, and that included Anne. This frustrated him. But whenever Anne's name was mentioned, we knew she was special. "You are loved," he said to her occasionally.

SATURDAY, OCTOBER 15

Mark fights his sit-up times. When his therapist told me that, in anger, he wrote, "My butt hurts," I knew he must have hurt all over. In a new, candid way, he said exactly what he thought. "I felt it was sorta' funny, what he said," she told me, "but I asked Mark to re-phrase his statement."

He printed, "I want to lie down on the mat."

I believe Mark's humor is coming back, Lord.

◆   ◆   ◆

We slipped Mark's wool robe over his hospital gown and wheeled him out to the parking lot. With the aid of an orderly, the three of us transferred him from the wheelchair into our car and took him on his first trip away from the hospital. As Bob drove, I held Mark's head upright so no unexpected movement would jolt him. He didn't speak, although he looked intently in every direction at the deepening blush of autumn. When sitting up became painful, Mark tired and, unable to use the urinal, directed the retreat back to the hospital.

When we returned the wheelchair, the receptionist asked, "Was that Mark Laughlin?"

"Yes, he's our son."

She confided, "I've worked here for six years and no one has ever received more calls than Mark. Individuals are always asking about him."

SUNDAY, OCTOBER 16

Sixty-seven days after the accident, the last tube has been removed from Mark's body. "Freedom," Mark said pointing to his nose.

Approximately 40 members of the church college class visited Mark. They went in three or four at a time and stayed two or three minutes. Some touched him and others spoke words of encouragement assuring him of their prayers. Mark was exhausted afterwards but pleased about his visitors.

◆   ◆   ◆

Meanwhile, on her extensive trip to the Midwest and East coast, Kathy phoned Bob and me often and wrote Mark daily. I found reading and rereading these letters to Mark difficult because of his fragile emotions. Even so, her messages uplifted us:

• "May the Lord watch between you and me when we are absent one from the other" (Gen. 31:49, NASB). I pray that God will grant you strength and peace and a certainty of my love for you, even though I can't be there to tell you.

- A verse in church hit me this morning. God continues to build my faith as He heals you. Genesis 18:14a says, "Is anything too hard for the Lord? Of course not!"

- Doug and Mary Beth [close friends of Kathy's] will be encouraged to hear of your continued progress. They have been faithful to pray. God is answering!

TUESDAY, OCTOBER 18

Good news. They've stopped all Mark's medications! Now he takes no medications whatsoever-no antibiotics, no anti-seizure medication, no high blood pressure medicine. Praise You, Lord, he hasn't had any seizures.

When I told Mark I could understand all he'd said he replied, "That's encouraging." But he cried when Bob left on a five-day trip.

◆   ◆   ◆

When my two sisters, their husbands, and a cousin visited Mark again, they watched him stand with the assistance of two therapists. What energy he expends! Mark struggled like a man possessed. After a few moments, my older brother-inlaw stepped outside the room.

During the afternoon Mark's learning continued. He identified objects as I flashed picture cards, but he couldn't name two objects new to him-"commode" and "urinal."

Throughout the afternoon, whenever we reviewed the cards he identified every object except those two. Distraught and tearful, in his soft, slow voice Mark kept repeating, "I'm dumb. I'm stupid." Finally, I understood what he was saying: "Night nurse...won't let me use...urinal or commode. Have to say...right word first."

I was fired up and ready for an encounter. To Mark I said, "Let's call the nurse in charge."

"Yeah," he responded, and touched the call button.

Bustling in, the day nurse asked, "How can I help you?"

"Mark has a problem," I replied, "with the night nurse."

Mark pointed to the two flash cards.

After the conversation, although weepy, Mark felt better. The nurse assured him the situation would never happen again.

I made a joke of it, too, by writing the words "Urinal" and "Commode" in large letters on tag board and taping it to Mark's closet door.

"That's kinda' stupid," Mark said, grinning.

"I think it's kinda' clever," I replied.

Later, Mark pressed his call button, proud that he now had enough strength in his left hand to light up the signal.

A nurse came into his room. "Urinal, please," he said as he pointed to the words.

"That's no joke, either."

SATURDAY, OCTOBER 22

Two of our son's close friends sent a card that read, "This get-well card has not been touched by human hands." On the inside was a picture of a gorilla wearing a nurse's cap. "I had the night nurse pick it out for you."

Lord, we needed that laugh. But we won't display the card.

◆   ◆   ◆

On his usual evening rounds, Dr. Markham said, "Mark, you're making good progress. Your Dad and Mom can move you to RIO next Monday."

TUESDAY, OCTOBER 25

Today, with anguish and glory, Mark took two faltering steps with his left leg. Each time the right leg was advanced by the therapist. Mark also raised his right leg into a bent position.

Bit by bit, my medication is lifting my depression. Thank You, Lord, for these answers to prayer.

◆   ◆   ◆

A friend who stopped by regularly asked Mark about his spiritual life. He scolded our son for not reading the Word, ignoring the fact that Mark couldn't hold a book or remember what he read. He didn't listen to tapes or the radio or watch TV because the information was presented too fast for him to interpret. The unfair, self-righteous reprimand haunted Mark. He was defenseless.

WEDNESDAY, OCTOBER 26

Lord, I'm saddened about Mark's discussion with Anne regarding her commitment to him. They both are hurting.

Anne was kind to me when she stated, "We'll re-evaluate our relationship when Mark's well." Then, as if it were an afterthought, she said, "I think maybe you shouldn't introduce me as Mark's special friend anymore."

Lord, I have grown to love Anne. The sudden change leaves an emptiness within me. Mark needs her. I need her, too.

THURSDAY, OCTOBER 27

Lord, Mark does have some recall and I'm so grateful. Of the several nurses who greeted Mark when we visited 4R he looked at Shirley Berglund intently and said, "I remember you." She gets my vote for "Nurse of the Year."

◆   ◆   ◆

After a nurse dressed Mark in his clothes, we went for a drive. On this momentous trip, we drove to RIO and introduced Mark to what would be his new residence.

Pushing his wheelchair into the hall, into the therapy room, and into a patient's room, we watched for Mark's reactions. With his usual aphasic language he remarked, frowning, "The facility doesn't have long, bright corridors for my nightly wheelchair strolls."

On the way back we stopped by our church. Greeting Pastor highlighted Mark's outing. "We had a terrific time," Mark told the nurses after he returned.

SATURDAY, OCTOBER 29

In his rehab room the call button gives Mark some control over his tiny space. Yet, Bob found Mark in agony for three consecutive, early-morning visits. The call button hadn't been left on his chest where his left hand could reach it. His faint cries for the urinal went unheeded. Bob quickly told the orderly the first time. The second time, he was upset, to say the least. This morning Bob confronted the orderly sternly.

"Please don't tell anyone," the orderly pleaded. "It won't happen again."

◆   ◆   ◆

This morning I stayed with Mark instead of going to church. Shortly after arriving I turned on our radio church program. "We've been praying for Mark for weeks since his tragic bicycle accident," Pastor said. "I wish all of you could have had the experience I had yesterday of seeing Mark's big grin. His face mirrored the work of God in his life."

While Mark and I listened with full hearts the congregation sang, "There Is Power in the Name of Jesus."

"Let's take a few moments and praise God for what He's doing in Mark's life." Pastor added, "Every once in a while we have the gracious privilege of glimpsing that power in action. Enable us, Heavenly Father, to be perpetually grateful to praise You for what is happening day by day.

"Thank you that Mark is improving…Heavenly Father, we pray you will restore him completely and to the ministry to which he's been called."

SUNDAY, OCTOBER 30

I found out this afternoon that daily the speech therapist used the Ezekiel chart. She trained Mark in pronouncing two or three syllables at a time while exercising breath control.

God, how great of You to plan for Mark to reread those encouraging truths. I believe, by divine intervention, You reached out to Mark in the fog.

Whenever these loving statements seem to contradict present circumstances I remind myself that You, Lord are dispelling our fears.

I know, God, You carry me through day by day. The Bible truths we've learned through the years are helping us in our darkness. Our goal still is to make You visible to others.

I've been at the bottom and You were already there waiting for me. It's solid. Now I'm on the rebound and Mark is ready to move to RIO tomorrow.

11

Moved To Rio

○ ○

What have we to expect? Anything.
What have we to hope? Everything.
What have we to fear? Nothing.

—Edward B. Pusey

Mark found it difficult saying farewell that morning to the Providence Hospital staff who had provided him superb care. He cried without restraint.

The RIO staff members, wearing Halloween costumes, greeted Mark. Bewildered by their gaiety and celebration of the holiday, he stared intensely at his new helpers. Already overwhelmed by exchanging the known for the unknown, Mark frowned frequently and appeared troubled.

Dr. Gary Ward, a physiatrist (a rehabilitation medicine specialist), examined Mark. A cordial, approachable professional, he headed the team involved with Mark's care.

Mark loathed the move. To compound his trouble, during the afternoon he was left alone in the bathroom and fell between the toilet and the wall. Afterward, through sobs, he told Bob and me what happened. "No one heard my calls. Even if they had, they couldn't understand because I slur my words. A nurse found me after what seemed like an eternity."

Although he was not hurt physically, the incident created a deep-rooted fear.

I thought, *Did the nurse not know that Mark lacked balance?* Bob quickly checked with the nursing staff clarifying Mark's limitations. We hoped this would not happen again.

Looking at Mark, one would never suspect that our son toppled without supports. He looked normal. How terrifying and demoralizing not to be able to help himself even for personal hygiene care. Mark had been forced to give up all dignity. I ached for him.

Yet, his right arm reached higher. His right leg showed more mobility. We counted the positives, but Mark's lack of emotional control was the hardest problem for us to cope with. Many of his reactions were overblown and at times he lacked sound judgment. We reminded ourselves that the accident had damaged Mark's emotional center (emotional lability).

Over the weekend I had labeled Mark's personal belongings. The nurses dressed Mark daily, but I looked forward to when he'd be able to dress himself. Each evening, before bidding Mark good night, he selected, and I lay out the clothing he would wear the next day. Mark also enjoyed choosing his soft diet menu. All these accomplishments were tiny steps forward.

MONDAY, OCTOBER 31

Mark's move is proving traumatic. But, Lord, thanks for the ray of sunshine when Kathy called from New York. It's exciting to know that she canceled a couple of interviews at medical schools that weren't her top choices to be here two days early.

I think Mark should greet Kathy at the airport. Don't You think so, too?

◆   ◆   ◆

Today after assisting Mark with his meal, Bob signaled me to come out in the hall. "This morning Mark was despondent and sobbed." He told me, 'I've been told I'll never walk.'"

Bob continued, "I talked with staff members and found what was troubling Mark. The physical therapist told him, he'd probably never use the walker again.

"What else will he combat?" I asked. "It's one hit after another."

Later we found out. Through tears, Mark told us, "A nurse left me alone in the shower. I fell off the shower chair." He stopped to take a deep breath, and then went on. "There was water all over. I swallowed, and choked. No one heard me calling. I thought I was going to drown, but finally a nurse came. Although his emotions were shattered, he suffered no physical injury.

We confronted this nurse, barely holding in our rage. She apologized profusely saying, "I'm very sorry. I got so busy I forgot about him, but it won't happen again. Please forgive me."

Bob and I could only hope that she would live up to her promise.

TUESDAY, NOVEMBER 1

Day two, strike two. Lord, did we make the right choice? Things must get better. Mark is being ripped apart emotionally. He cries all the time. He has so little sense of security. Please give him relief from this unrelenting misery.

◆   ◆   ◆

Mark's desire to walk overshadowed needs like improving his speech and physical-mental agility. The RIO team approach to his walking began with specific needs. "First, he must learn to balance his torso. Then he won't need a walker," said his therapist.

Meanwhile Bob obtained permission for Mark's early evening airport outing. We asked the staff to keep Kathy's arrival secret. Mark didn't need more emotional upheaval.

WEDNESDAY, NOVEMBER 2

Kathy called again from New York, frustrated. She's missed her plane because of a delayed taxi connection. She'll arrive this evening at 9:30 p.m. How glad I am that we've said nothing to Mark about greeting her at the airport.

◆   ◆   ◆

When I arrived to assist Mark with his evening meal, his nurse apologized. "I blurted out to Mark the good news about going to the airport. I guess I was just too excited."

Mark was so psyched he could hardly contain himself. However, we obtained reluctant staff approval for Mark's later outing, way past his bedtime.

By the time we pushed Mark in his wheelchair into the lobby, a half-hour delay was posted. As the minutes ticked by his discomfort mounted. Then a second 30-minute postponement was announced. We endured that, too. Finally, Mark, weary and fidgeting, said, "I hurt and gotta' go to bed." But Bob helped him stand for a minute as I adjusted his pillows.

At last the plane landed. We swelled with excitement as we saw Kathy walk up the ramp toward us. Mark's head tilted upward, and he wailed tears of joy. Kathy gently wrapped him in her deep embrace, wordless. Then, as she wheeled him down the airport corridor, he basked in her undivided attention while she beamed with pleasure over his progress.

That evening as we tucked Mark into his bed, he whispered, "This has been a great day."

WEDNESDAY, NOVEMBER 2 (Cont.)

Yes, Lord, this has been a wonderful day. Kathy's enthusiasm over Mark's progress excited Bob and me. How wonderful that Mark could greet her.

Tonight, we can only say…thank You.

◆   ◆   ◆

Mark's gradual improvement earned him permission to come home on weekends. What a spine-tingler having him scheduled for a 48-hour leave. We then received homecare training.

THURSDAY, NOVEMBER 3

It's an understatement to say that Mark's accident has made a radical change in our priorities. Because so many friends have provided meals for us, I've only shopped at the dairy drive-in since his accident.

Having left work early I felt like I was walking on air. What fun to do something so ordinary again, shopping for food and medical supplies.

◆   ◆   ◆

That evening Bob and I bubbled with excitement. After work, for the first time in three months, I drove directly home while Bob drove to RIO to pick up Mark.

The long-awaited moment arrived when Bob drove into the driveway. As I watched from the nook window, Mark's emotions erupted. He was home again. We both cried tears of joy.

A neighbor assisted Bob in lifting Mark, in his wheelchair, into our house. Overpowered by his jubilant homecoming, Mark regained his composure while lying on the couch watching a crackling fire in the fireplace. Quietly, Bob and I took Mark's hands as we thanked God for His goodness and reveled in being home. Together!

I had prepared the guest bedroom by purchasing a night-light and equipping the bedside stand with a urinal and call-bell. Mark appeared content and secure when we transferred him into bed. The next morning we awoke realizing Mark had not rung for us. He was delighted!

FRIDAY, NOVEMBER 4

Lord, You know that Dr. Markham told us, "When Mark goes home, he'll need 24-hour nursing care." How grateful we are that You intervened and this prophecy, also, wasn't true. I'm overwhelmed and thank You.

◆   ◆   ◆

Bob had screwed in two heavy-duty metal rings, one on each side of the cupboard, below the kitchen sink. A taut strap, which hooked into the rings, went around Mark's hips holding him firm and upright. Twice daily, Mark stood on a wooden wedge, his toes positioned higher than his heels, for 20 minutes. This stance helped correct the contracture of Mark's feet. The right foot now dropped 27 degrees below a right angle. We hoped this stressful exercise would become more tolerable with practice.

SATURDAY, NOVEMBER 5

The task of lifting Mark in and out of the bathtub takes all the strength Bob and I can exert. Yet, Mark has complete confidence in our transferring him from his wheelchair for bathing or onto the toilet.

◆   ◆   ◆

Mark had mentioned that his beard would disappear when he could shave himself. Sunday morning, with my assistance, he laboriously took several shaving strokes, rested, made several more strokes, and finally shaved off the heavy, thick whiskers. The arduous task left him perspiring. But he said, "I'm pleased," as he lay down to rest and listen to our church program on the radio. Mark looked thin and frail without his full, reddish beard, but more like himself.

When it was time to return to RIO, Mark, choking back tears, said, "This whole thing makes me mad."

"That's okay, Mark. I know it's hard," Kathy replied soothingly.

My medication made me feel better, but being responsible for Mark's care over the weekend drained me. Bob and I decided I would not accompany Mark when he returned to RIO on Sunday evenings. When Mark realized

I was not going to RIO, too, he cried. Immediately I decided it was far less stressful to accompany Mark than to feel the pain of seeing him cry.

SUNDAY, NOVEMBER 6

This evening, not long after Bob and I returned home, Mark called us for the first time. "I've raised my right arm above my head."
    "Great job, Mark," I said.
    What fabulous news, Lord. Thanks for a weekend of many miracles.

MONDAY, NOVEMBER 7

Mark was weepy again. Lord, his emotional lability hits me at the center of my being. How much more this must plague Mark. Please help him.

TUESDAY, NOVEMBER 8

We took Mark his hiking boots. He will wear them to support his ankles. Mark said, "I'm standing straighter and with help I walked 70 feet today."
    We praise You, Lord.

◆   ◆   ◆

Our RIO team presented an evaluation of Mark's status and discussed with Bob, Kathy, and me their treatment goals. They recited an intimidating list of Mark's problems:

• lacked sufficient balance reflexes;

• took twice the normal time to perform hand functions;

• had a paralyzed soft palate;

• had spasticity which would decrease as his motor control increased;

• had contractures of both feet with more in the right foot and had some contracture in his right shoulder; and

• had several cognitive-processing weaknesses:

    a shortened attention span;

    difficulty with new learning and recall;

    a trace of aphasia; and

some anomia (inability to remember names), and difficulty in generalizing, abstracting, and problem solving.

"The correction for the contracture of Mark's feet will be completed in steps," said the physical therapist. "Mark will receive new casts periodically until the contractures are eliminated." Her confidence cheered me.

Dr. Ward stated, "Mark undergoes six hours of therapy daily. He rests from the arduous schedule on weekends, but you should help him with the passive exercises. Make sure he stands on the slanted board twice daily." In addition, he said, "Every day, Mark should perform 80 inhalations on the spirometer, to strengthen his airflow for improved speaking ability."

The staff also discussed inserting a palate lift to help Mark speak more clearly. Later, surgery for correcting the paralysis would be considered.

Lord, please heal the palatal paralysis, too.

Since the clinical psychologist felt Mark was improving exceptionally well, she tested Mark for only 30 minutes rather than six hours. "I'm amazed at Mark's improvement," she said.

WEDNESDAY, NOVEMBER 9

Lord, the staff's confidence that Mark can be helped is great news. He's come so much farther than the doctors ever predicted. Philippians 4:6,7 perfectly reflects how we feel: "Do not be anxious about anything, but in everything, by prayer and petition, with thanksgiving, present your requests to God. And the peace of God, which transcends all understanding, will guard your hearts and minds in Christ Jesus."

We believe, Lord, that You will continue Mark's healing journey.

Mark reported, "I'm standing straighter, I'm walking better, and I'm glad I moved to RIO!"

Did I hear this right, Lord? That's music to my ears.

◆   ◆   ◆

Mark's emotions continued like a yo-yo. When up, he became over-elated and knew he would walk again, probably tomorrow. When down, he lapsed into a pool of despair where he was sure he would never walk again.

On an upswing, Mark set another goal for himself: "I want to attend church on Christmas Sunday, using crutches. I won't go to church in this wheelchair."

That evening the therapist drove several wheelchair patients to a Trailblazer basketball game. Mark went and took his urinal that had painted on the side, "Go, Blazers, Go!"

Bob and I also attended the game and sat close enough to observe Mark. We noticed his short attention span. He could perform only one task at a time. When eating popcorn, he concentrated on picking up the kernel and placing it in his mouth. He couldn't follow the continuous, fast play. As time went on he became even more exhausted.

After the game, worried about Mark, we stopped by RIO. Sure enough, he was back in the pit. With deep, hysterical sobs he cried, "I'll never walk. I'll never, never walk again."

"Mark, you are walking," Bob said.

"You are improving each day," I added.

Despite Bob's prayer with Mark, our son's anxiety wasn't eased and we finally left him in despair. As we drove home Bob said, "It's hard to believe Mark will ever be normal again."

"We must pray with faith, believing," I responded. And, yet, I wondered, too.

SATURDAY, NOVEMBER 12

Mark wrote a tender letter expressing gratitude to the third grade class in San Francisco for their prayers and letters. He also answered letters from friends. These little triumphs ease our hearts and let us know You hear our cries.

Lord, I thank You that I'm not having to ask Mark to repeat what he says as often. We notice considerable improvement in his speech.

SUNDAY, NOVEMBER 13

Mark was upset when Bob left for church this morning. "I wish I were able to go, too," he said. Mark, however, listened to Pastor's sermon on the radio and then, on his own, read a chapter in the book of Mark, the first time since the accident he had picked up and was able to hold his Bible.

We had our first morning free of tears.

◆   ◆   ◆

This afternoon Mark, while still lying on the couch, counseled and prayed with his young alcoholic friend, Cary.

Later, Mark told me, "He opened up because I've become vulnerable." Breaking into tears, Mark added, "I made the right decision. I'm exhausted, but I helped my friend."

During the evening, while playing games with his friends, Mike and Kim, Mark told them that he had ministered to his alcoholic friend, and that he had talked to two nurses about Christ. They were amazed to hear of these dramatic moves. Mark was reaching beyond himself.

TUESDAY, NOVEMBER 15

The pain of our crisis remains deep, but I'm grateful we could talk with Mark about Job and the parallels we see to Mark's personal Gethsemane. Lord, as Mark's former abilities return help us appreciate what he can do rather than lament what he can't yet do.

WEDNESDAY, NOVEMBER 16

Eleven friends visited Mark. When the last person left, he was exhausted. I'm thankful Lord, that the staff is molding new foot casts for Mark.

FRIDAY, NOVEMBER 18

Mark phoned me at the bank for the first time since his hospitalization. I've never received a more welcomed call. "Hi, Mom. This is Mark."

This is my boy returning to me. I'm sure my face shone all day.

Mark is home for the weekend again. He prefers eating Friday dinner at home rather than RIO. He said, "Mom, your cookin's better."

◆   ◆   ◆

While I was shopping this afternoon Anne had stopped by. She had left before I returned, but Mark was upset. He confided that he had talked about their commitment to each other. "Anne responded kindly," Mark said, "but she doesn't feel about me the way I feel about her."

Because Mark now remembered details, the shock of this encounter devastated him.

Mark felt dreadful, too, when we told him he'd previously brought up the topic with Anne. Through tears he said, "I must apologize to her."

SUNDAY, NOVEMBER 20

I helped Mark wash his hair while he was supported against the cupboard at the kitchen sink. But what a chore. Mark found it difficult bending his head down far enough. We had more water on the counter and the floor than on his head.

That faithful twosome, Mike and Kim, were here again this evening. Lord, what would we do without them? Thanks for revealing Your love to Mark through them. I'm grateful that Mark won his share of the number games.

MONDAY, NOVEMBER 21

After visiting Mark at RIO, it was a privilege to attend Bible study for the first time in over three months. It was a tonic for my soul as I realized how far Mark has advanced in his healing. Among those dear, faithful friends, I realized how blessed we were.

WEDNESDAY, NOVEMBER 23

Mark has a four-day Thanksgiving break at home. He's excited that Bob's family is coming for our annual Thanksgiving dinner, even more special this year.

What thrilling news, Lord, that the speech therapist reported Mark's aphasia is minor and he has only a trace of anomia. He disguises his deficit well.

And the greatest news of all: Social Worker, Susan Swanson, said, "Mark used to have 1,000,000 choices and he now has 750,000 choices." Lord, that Peter walked on the water was no miracle. See, I'm walking on air.

◆   ◆   ◆

Mark wanted to walk to the festive dinner table-not go in his wheelchair-so he stood up and placed his hands on Bob's shoulders. Mark moved cautiously. Taking slow, wobbly steps, he finally reached the dinner table while the others watched and cheered him on. Still, he couldn't eat and talk at the same time. Wearied by the labor-intensive job of eating, he said, "I'm exhausted." We assisted him in the toilsome journey back to the couch where he collapsed and remained in a somber mood the rest of the day.

FRIDAY, NOVEMBER 25

A pre-planned, short outing to the Oregon Museum of Science and Industry proved too much for Mark. The information was too technical. We stayed too long. The challenges presented and the energy expended shattered his fragile state of well-being. Lord, we made a mistake, but know You understand.

SATURDAY, NOVEMBER 26

Mark transferred from his wheelchair to a nook chair without assistance. His eating of the soft diet improves, although food still drops from his fork.

"I want to be normal like you two," he stammered when a bite of his pie fell in his lap.

I ached for Mark, but didn't want to give him pity.

SUNDAY, NOVEMBER 27

Mike and Kim were here for their usual Sunday evening visit. They never disappointed Mark who looked forward to chatting and playing number and word games with them. Then Mark became weepy because he had to return to RIO.

Mike wrapped his arms around Mark and said, "Don't be embarrassed, brother. I love you and care that you hurt." Kim softly agreed.

Mike and Kim are another of Mark's many affirmations from You, Lord, and I thank You. Your hugs strengthen me and increase my faith.

12

The Christmas Walk

○ ○

Miracles are not contrary to nature, but only contrary to what we know about nature.

—*Augustiine of Hippo*

THURSDAY, DECEMBER 1

Mark has to keep a diary as a speech assignment at RIO. Today he penned, "This morning I felt very discouraged. My right leg does not move well. I really want to attend Hinson Church on Christmas. That's less than four weeks away. God can answer my requests. Perhaps I need to trust more confidently."

With Mark's permission I often read his diary entries. This one moved me to pray: Lord, help us all to trust You for the fulfillment of Mark's goal.

FRIDAY, DECEMBER 2

Mark never loses sight of his goal of walking into church on Christmas morning. Though grateful for his courage, at times his driving ambition plagues me; I don't want Mark to be devastated should he not reach his objective.

After walking at RIO without the approval of his therapist, Mark made an entry in his diary. "Today I sinned. I stood next to my bed. I trembled. Eternity seemed to stand still. I walked. I made it to the wheelchair. I was ecstatic!"

The nurses now house Mark's canes at their station.

When Mark walked, we had to remind him to stand erect. If he didn't, I couldn't control his balance or hold him upright with the waist strap. Fortunately, Mark had never fallen, but he scowled when I asked him to stand erect.

Bob and I discussed again whether I could continue to assist Mark with his walking; I feared I couldn't keep him from falling. When Mark realized how hard he was making it for me, he apologized. "I'll quit acting that way," he said.

SATURDAY, DECEMBER 3

With my assistance Mark slowly pulled a polo shirt over his head; then he pulled a sock onto his left foot. And while I steadied him, he pulled his trousers on and zipped them, also. He perspired. This task was like a day's labor.

"Great job," I repeatedly say. Mark always smiles.

◆   ◆   ◆

Although the slow learning procedures left Mark perspiring, he persisted. Thinking through each basic procedure, Mark slowly established patterns for relearning former habits.

Gradually we introduced Mark to outside surroundings, preparing him for his Christmas goal. With Anne, we ventured out for her belated birthday dinner.

Fortunately the restaurant was convenient for maneuvering Mark's wheelchair and the meal was superb. Mark could not participate in the table talk and eat at the same time, but he did his best, practicing his returning social skills. Anne puzzled us because she avoided any conversation or eye contact with Mark during the evening. He knew he was left out.

After our return home Mark said, "I'm very sad. A special chapter in my life has ended, but I hope Anne and I stay friends." Mark went to bed disheartened and emotionally derailed.

Later, Bob asked, "How could Anne have been so insensitive? Can I forgive her?"

I ached for Mark, too. His mental anguish was now matched with his emotional pain.

SUNDAY, DECEMBER 4

Mark fell between the couch and a chair while lurching for the newspaper. Although shaken emotionally, he wasn't hurt. After much struggle, with an energy surge I lifted Mark off the floor. As I helped him to the couch he protested, "You know I've taken steps at RIO without a problem."

But he reluctantly promised not to walk unassisted.

TUESDAY, DECEMBER 6

Mel and El Jensen visited Mark tonight.

Mark demonstrated his abilities: sitting, standing, and taking two steps unassisted. Together we sang "God Is So Good." Our quintet's enthusiasm made up for our lack of quality. I loved hearing Mark sing again even though the injury had left him with limited pitch control and narrow vocal range.

◆   ◆   ◆

We often played number and letter games to rebuild Mark's learning skills. Showing no loss in math, he preferred playing number games. He feared letter games because he struggled finding the right words. Slowly, we introduced Boggle, Password, Scrabble, The Ungame, and Clue, but when these games proved too stressful, we reverted to his first choices.

WEDNESDAY, DECEMBER 7

Mark told me, "David asked if I'd mind if he dated Anne. I was hurt, but said he could."

I hugged Mark. "I'm sorry for your pain. This makes me sad, too."

THURSDAY, DECEMBER 8

Mark's friend, David, also called me seeking my approval for him to date Anne. I quickly thought of David's mother, Ruth Ann, my best friend. How could I keep our friendship and still be true to Mark? Finally, I said, "David, if my blessing matters, you have it." Privately, I had released Anne, but I didn't yet feel the words I'd spoken. I had often heard Mark tell Anne, "You are loved."

◆   ◆   ◆

For their first venture since the accident, Kathy and Mark went to a shopping mall.

Kathy reported, "We searched the complex for wheelchair access but there was none. I finally wheeled Mark's chair parallel to the sidewalk and helped him stand. While he clung to a frosty, metal pole with his bare hands, I quickly yanked the wheelchair onto the walk. After clearing this hurdle, he slumped back into the seat and we blended into the shopping mass."

After returning home, drained of energy, Mark's successful shopping trip was soon overshadowed by a cloud of despair.

"I feel like a child in my thinking," Mark said while writing notes on his Christmas cards. "If I had to write about the world, it would only take a paragraph. I'll never be normal again."

"Mark, you realized that your friend, Cary, could confide in you about his problem with alcohol because you, too, have lost major control of your life through your accident. Your comment was adult thinking," Kathy said.

Later, while looking at his face in a family portrait, Mark said, "I feel like a retarded shadow of my former self." His face was masked with tears. "Mark, you aren't," I said, hugging him. "You're a sharp, young man and dearly loved."

SATURDAY, DECEMBER 10

I know the importance of allowing Mark to express his grief. But his sorrow deepens my heartache. However, years of walking with You Lord, helps me. I must cling to facts, encourage Mark, and not rely on my unstable emotions.

FROM MARK'S CHRISTMAS CARD TO CBA, SATURDAY, DECEMBER 10th

"I feel a special glow as I write this card; your articles about me are appreciated. I feel much better and hope to walk [with canes] by Christmas. I'm looking forward to that occasion and hope you have a special Christmas, also."

SUNDAY, DECEMBER 11

Lord, what a monumental accomplishment for Mark, with Bob's help, to walk down to his room. I'm overjoyed for Mark's feat and yet after four months I still must work through forgiving those who initially failed Mark.

TUESDAY, DECEMBER 13

Mark is beside himself and doesn't know why he cries. I think maybe he is having some side effects from a muscle relaxant Dr. Ward prescribed.

THURSDAY, DECEMBER 15

Bob and I have an appointment with Pastor to discuss Mark's church attendance on Christmas. Lord, I'm so excited.

◆   ◆   ◆

Mark and Kathy planned another family outing. We belatedly celebrated Bob's birthday by dining at his favorite seafood restaurant. Mark enjoyed the delicious shrimp and, with great effort, was able to participate in some simple conversation and eat at the same time. While he and Kathy talked, Bob and I reveled in their chatter. We occasionally joined in the conversation.

We capped off the evening at the Willamette Repertory Theater. Kathy made arrangements with the personnel so Mark received first-class attention. An usher quickly transferred him from his wheelchair into an aisle seat. Mark enjoyed the "Christmas Carol."

FRIDAY, DECEMBER 16

In each successive outing we feel more confident Mark will reach his goal of going to church on Christmas Sunday without his wheelchair.

◆   ◆   ◆

Mark made a trial run to church on December 17th. Our church administrator opened the doors. Using canes and with Bob holding the waist strap, Mark entered the auditorium by a side door, a long, plodding walk from the street. Gazing with awe around a sanctuary in which he hadn't worshipped in over four months, he slumped into a pew. He then trudged 150 feet into his College Hall classroom where he again sat, exhausted.

Mark slowly returned to the car with a tired, trailing right foot, his successful venture overshadowing his weariness. "I'll be in church on Christmas day," he mused.

"We know you will, son," Bob replied.

SUNDAY, DECEMBER 18

Our Bible study group met in our home. Excitedly, they greeted Mark. "What a miracle you are," they exclaimed. Another great day! No tears.

MONDAY, DECEMBER 19

Mark received an encouraging message from a deaconess: "We are certainly reminded of our miracle-working God. Surely He has worked that for you. We feel certain that you'll attend church all aglow on Christmas. You'll be the brightest, most sparkling decoration there is. We can hardly wait."

Lord, our excitement is mounting.

WEDNESDAY, DECEMBER 21

Once a week RIO's recreational therapists sponsored a family night, but Mark had never attended, unsure of his ability to talk with others. To our delight, Mark went to the Christmas party. To top off the evening, Santa arrived. With childlike glee, Mark received three gifts from Santa's helpers. What progress!

◆   ◆   ◆

Bob, Kathy, and I listened while Mark's rehab team reviewed his progress at RIO.

Dr. Ward stated, "We agree Mark can become an outpatient in early January if he has a trained assistant. Our team will help you prepare for his home move and train his attendant."

Kathy quietly intervened, "I have all of my required courses completed for my medical degree in June. I'd like to be my brother's attendant until leaving for Zaire in March."

Mark, who was wheeled into the conference room in time to hear Kathy's offer, beamed.

Surprised, grateful, and relieved, I hugged Kathy.

THURSDAY, DECEMBER 22

On Mark's checkout sheet was typed:

NEEDED:

*   One adult wheelchair for outdoor, long distance trips for three months, option to buy.

    (I thought, he will not need it longer than three months.)

*   One insert for the right shoe for ankle support needed for a lifetime. (Yes, I can handle that.)

*   Two lumex straight canes needed for a lifetime.

    That brought me up short, and then I thought,

    (No, God, I can't believe that.)

FRIDAY, DECEMBER 23

There was a knock at our door and then we heard caroling above the howl of the wind and snow hitting the house. Two church families who regularly prayed for Mark had come to show their love for us. We ushered them in out of the cold so that they could get warm. Each of the five children and their parents (my "angel nurse" one of them) warmed our hearts with their carols. Mark smiled and thanked each one and hugged the three pre-school children before they departed.

Lord, forgive me for ever doubting Your love.

◆   ◆   ◆

Kathy drove to our home at noon to share Christmas Eve and be on hand for Mark's big day. During the evening Mark, in a relaxed, confiding mood, said, "You know, I've had thoughts of suicide."

After a breathless silence, Kathy recovered her composure and asked, "What exactly did you think?"

"Oh, I felt depressed, but I hadn't planned how I'd do it," Mark replied.

Somehow Mark had made it possible for us to candidly express our deep, painful agony since the accident. Mark, Kathy, and I discussed how we denied or envisioned erasing the reality of the crisis. Bob was a passive participant. The other three of us hoped the honest discussion would be therapeutic and hasten our healing.

We enjoyed a quiet and thankful evening by a glowing fireside. We had purchased no presents; Mark was our Christmas. But he presented gifts to Kathy and me. We each opened small packages wrapped in holly paper Mark had designed. He had painted and glazed the mocha-colored mugs in occupational therapy, and they glistened with the word "coffee" printed in different languages. The tender moment overwhelmed us. We couldn't utter a word, but hugged Mark as his eyes danced with merriment.

Then the long awaited day arrived. Mark, with two canes and Bob's support, plodded to the church's side entrance, just as planned.

The church choir was practicing the morning anthem, "King of Love," as we entered the hallway and stood at the side entrance to the auditorium. Pastor hugged Mark and other staff members greeted him. A line of greeters going in for worship also flowed by.

One of our friends who hadn't felt able to visit Mark at the hospital hugged him. She began, "Oh, Mark," hesitated, cried, and then buried her head in his shoulder.

We seated ourselves at a side pew, easy for Mark to reach, and soon the church service began. At the conclusion of the anthem Pastor spoke. "After the thank you of 'King of Love' there is one other thank you we'd like to lift to our Lord today. On August 9, Mark Laughlin was injured. We remember those first hours of uncertainty as, on August 11, he was rushed into emergency surgery with very severe brain damage. The whole church family has rallied"...

"We remember in those early days we prayed first that he might live.…
And then we prayed for the return of his faculties. Since that day in August we
have been praying and God has been working. We have a special Christmas
gift for the family today.

"Mark, will you stand? Welcome home."

A great communal intake of breath rippled through the congregation.
Prolonged, spontaneous applause broke out. I did not see a dry eye in the
sanctuary.

"Wave at them, Mark," Pastor urged, smiling. To the congregation he
added, "You can't know what it meant the first day we saw that arm lifted
in a wave.

"He isn't completely recovered yet. He walks with two canes, but he has
been practicing for weeks in order to be with you on Christmas day. This is
his first time back in church. I think we need to thank God for that, don't
you? It's a tremendous, wonderful answer to prayer.

"We thank You, Father, for the way You have given Mark back to us. We
pray now for complete recovery…May our faith be increased"

The service continued but, as I looked at Mark, I could see that he couldn't
keep up with the lyrics being sung. He glanced around the auditorium,
thumbed through the hymnal, and looked at the church bulletin. I knew
that for him Pastor's message and the entire service seemed to be on fast-
forward.

When the service closed, more friends welcomed Mark. We also stayed
for the beginning of the 11:00 a.m. service and departed after Pastor's
comments about Mark. The eyes of the congregation were glued on our son
as he struggled up the steps and out of the sanctuary. Accompanied by Kathy,
he attended the College Class where the youth minister enveloped him with
an emotional hug.

By the time we reached home, freezing rain blanketed our street. With
extreme caution, the three of us assisted Mark into the house.

Safely deposited on the sofa, Mark said, "I was terrified and overwhelmed
by the sea of faces." Then he added, "I'm worn out but excited that I reached
my goal."

SUNDAY, DECEMBER 25

Many, oh so many, people had been praying. No wonder Mark made it
to church. My angel nurse wrote, "My little preschoolers and I continue
to pray for you faithfully five times a day: three meals, naptime, and
bedtime. They won't let me forget. Your progress is such a tribute to the
greatness of God!"

Our yearly Christmas dinner, with the Tidswell family as our guests, added another blessed touch to our already glorious day. How thankful we were for the gift of His Son, and that He was giving Mark back to us, too.

Filled with joy, the start of our holiday season surpassed all our expectations.

Lord, this is one of the happiest moments of my life.

13

Tender Loving Care

○ ○

I dressed his wounds, God healed him.

—Ambroise Pare

After the Christmas break Susan Berkman, a deaconess with special training in language skills, would tutor Mark in speech and language development, completing his program.

Kathy would drive Mark to RIO's outpatient physical therapy three times a week and to speech therapy twice weekly. She would monitor his home-therapy program on weekdays. Bob and I would be available early morning, after work, and weekends to help Mark with the "dailyness" of living. Together, we made quite a team.

TUESDAY, DECEMBER 27

How we all had the nerve to venture out of town I'll never know. We bundled Mark up and off we drove to the beach. When we arrived at our condo, Mark surprised us. With Bob's support, he toiled up two flights of stairs.

Lord, thanks for this victory, too.

◆　　　　◆　　　　◆

Travel discomforts and distance from Mark's medical team concerned us. Unfortunately, Mark had a cold that worsened. Worried about her brother's weak cough reflexes, Kathy called Dr. Ward. Upon his counsel, Kathy and I alternated turning Mark onto his stomach every three hours. I took the day shift, Kathy the night shift. With the edge of our cupped hands we repeated a constant, gentle chopping motion over his upper back. This loosened the mucous, preventing congestion from settling in Mark's lungs.

THURSDAY, DECEMBER 29

Mark's vitality waned. We played some table games. But during most of the day Mark lay on the couch, lamented his losses, cried and, at times, dozed.

SATURDAY, DECEMBER 31

We drove home this morning. The weekend was tear-ridden and Mark is physically weak. But I'm pleased, Lord, that he's feeling good about the trip.

◆   ◆   ◆

On New Year's Day Mark attended his second church service. Under sunny skies, he handled his canes with more ease as he slowly trudged into church.

In his sermon, Pastor said, "In His present exalted position…Jesus is over all…. Nothing touches the child of God except by permission of our sovereign Lord. If He is sovereign, there is nothing that will reach me without His permission…

"It was so nice to go through the past year with Bob, Milli, Kathy, and Mark Laughlin. They realized that Jesus was sovereign. What happened to Mark happened because God permitted it. I am sure that He didn't cause it. But He allowed it."

Bob, Kathy, and I admitted we each had our doubts, but now our feelings more clearly affirmed the fact that God was in control.

MONDAY, JANUARY 2

With Kathy at his side, Mark returned to RIO, excited because he'll soon be home. Kathy quickly absorbed instructions for monitoring his outpatient program. We're thrilled that she can be her brother's caregiver.

You have provided so well for Mark, Lord.

◆   ◆   ◆

When Dr. Ward discharged Mark no words could adequately express our joy.

The RIO staff stressed the importance of the family getting away from the home setting, saying we needed relief from the emotional environment surrounding Mark's care. Kathy would arrive at 7:45 a.m. and leave when I returned from work.

After physical therapy on Fridays, Kathy and Mark would leisurely have lunch at a novelty restaurant. The diversion would temporarily take them beyond the stressful routine.

Mark was also invited to join the members of a church study group that had met at our home each Monday night prior to Mark's accident. Faithful prayers for Mark, they demonstrated their love and support. "You're the greatest miracle we've ever seen," they repeatedly told him.

FRIDAY, JANUARY 6

Mark leans upon Kathy and she identifies with her brother's hurts and needs. When he cries over his actual or perceived losses, she grieves with him. She lives 1 John 3:18:..."let us not love with words and tongues but with actions and in truth." Kathy's shared grief consoles Mark, but she tells me, "I still struggle with guilt and doubts."

◆   ◆   ◆

The struggle went on. After about ten days Kathy reported when I came home, "We had a very sad day." Mark had become distraught. The disparity between where he was and where he wanted to be distressed him. As Kathy left Mark turned to me and said, "I'm so discouraged about my walking." His eyes mirrored his sorrow.

That evening Mark startled us by asking, "What did they do with my brain?" Bob and I explained the large blood clot, the surgery, and the healing that was taking place. I stressed that, despite medical predictions, God was healing him. "That process is ongoing," I stated.

"Why has God allowed me to be placed on the shelf when I desire to be in seminary?" Mark then asked.

"I don't know, but God does. He is sovereign," I answered. We choked with emotion.

SUNDAY, JANUARY 15

Progress continues. After completing his floor exercises, Mark lurches and sways before coming to a standing position unassisted. With the aid of support bars and a handrail, he can step in and out of the shower without help. He walks with a cane with someone at his side, but doesn't need their physical support.

We thank You, Lord, for these giant steps.

THURSDAY, JANUARY 26

Last night Mark stayed up late and went to bed on his own. This morning he turned from his back onto his side, the first turn since his accident.

Lord, these victories thrill us.

◆   ◆   ◆

Mark ventured out to a movie with three friends. Returning, he walked into the house, weeping.

Knowing that this was a symptom of his ongoing emotional trauma, I prompted, "Mark, can you tell me how you feel?"

Gathering control he began, "It was hard to walk in the cold, snowy weather. I needed constant help so I wouldn't fall.

"I don't talk like others.

"I'm not normal.

"I'm weird and a misfit."

He stopped, swallowed hard, and shakily said, "No one sees the real me who is hurting."

My heart ached to see his pain as he continued.

"I try hard to listen and understand.

"I smile at everyone.

"I try to say the right things.

"I struggle, I agonize, and I wonder.

"That's my real world. It's very painful."

"Mark, we know that you're hurting. How else can we help?"

"Mom, I don't know. I just needed to vent," Mark said.

"Mark, this is part of your healing. To heal you must feel," I said as I hugged him.

SATURDAY, FEBRUARY 4

Dear God, show us how to share Mark's emotional pain. His anguish is indescribable and his suffering is so lonely. Why can't Mark ever walk away from the constant torment? It seems too hard for him to bear.

Even so, I am thankful he shows steady improvement. With Job, I say, "Even though you slay me yet I will trust in You."

SUNDAY, FEBRUARY 5

Mark, Bob, and I gave our testimonies at a college sing held at our home. Our hearts were so touched when over 30 members who filled our living room had a sharing and praise time. They extended spontaneous love to Mark. He soaked it up like a sponge. I could feel healing happening.

FRIDAY, FEBRUARY 10

With joyful hearts, Bob, Kathy, Mark, and I attended our church Valentine banquet. Mark, for the first time, put aside his hiking boots and wore his dress shoes. And Lord, what music to our ears to hear Mark exclaim, "This was a fun evening-and I walked well in my good shoes."

◆   ◆   ◆

When a deaconess brunch and praise session at our home featured Mark as their guest, Susan, his speech therapist, helped him feel at ease. Mark spoke to the group about his progress. In his closing comments he said, "I can't adequately express my appreciation for all your prayers. They are being answered." He paused, smiled, and added, "Don't stop now."

SATURDAY, FEBRUARY 11

How thankful I am for these 23 deaconesses who have constantly prayed for Mark. They have ministered to all of us by providing meals, sending cards, and calling. These thoughtful people, Lord, are a reflection of You. And thanks, too, for the praises and petitions for Mark that continue in the CBA News.

TUESDAY, FEBRUARY 14

Lord, it's been too heavy to bear or even write about. I know I've been in denial about the bank's solvency. The economic slump has been a key factor, but the FDIC audit even classified one of our director's huge loans. You know, too, Lord, that my initial concern about this director has deepened tension between Bob and me.

Bob and I are the bank's largest shareholders. We have the most to lose financially, but that doesn't bother me. What, if any, value I placed on money is gone-it can't heal Mark or buy peace of mind.

But, Lord, I ache for over 200 family members and friends who believed in our stewardship concept. I'm so embarrassed. Please, may the classified loans be paid and the needed capital come in.

SUNDAY, FEBRUARY 19

Leona Nettler, Mark's former Primary Sunday School Superintendent, waited after church to speak with him. A naturally dramatic person, she emotionally took his hand, looked into his eyes, and said, "I wanted to shake hands with a walking miracle."

Mark smiled.

Lord, we are enthralled by Leona's enthusiasm. I'm aware that Mark is a medical miracle and thank You.

◆   ◆   ◆

Mark remained on an emotional roller coaster. He acknowledged advancing more rapidly mentally than physically, but retaining information was difficult. Initially, Mark read assigned speech therapy articles twice, then underlined during the third reading. The fourth time he outlined the content. Now he combined activities by underlining during the initial reading and outlining the important points during the second reading.

Susan counseled Mark in addition to being an excellent tutor. She attentively listened, sensed his pain, and allowed him to vent his feelings.

SATURDAY, FEBRUARY 25

We ran away to our condo overnight. Mark, formerly a good swimmer, tried swimming. In the condo complex pool, he struggled in vain. His right leg and right arm couldn't perform the once automatic, natural strokes. In the pool beside him, Kathy and I tried to help, but nothing worked. Finally, after repeated attempts, and unwanted gulps of water, he admitted defeat. The reality oppressed him. We couldn't think of anything comforting to do or say.

◆   ◆   ◆

As Kathy's departure for Zaire drew near, Mark was also obsessed with two other concerns. "Kathy's taken great care of me. Who can replace her? And will she receive less recognition at graduation because she helped me instead of being in school?"

"Mark, we know God will provide. We're looking for another attendant for you. And we're confident that Kathy's kind act won't reflect negatively on her scholastic status."

◆   ◆   ◆

During the next Sunday morning service Pastor interviewed Kathy. He told the congregation, "Kathy Laughlin has been studying medicine at the Oregon Health Science University. She plans to spend some very important time in just the next two months." Turning to her, he asked, "Where are you going and what will you be doing, Kathy?"

"On March 25 I will leave for two months in Zaire…I will be helping with the medical work, rounding on patients, assisting in surgery, and helping in outpatient clinics.…"

"Kathy, I remember when your brother was injured. It was a time of trauma for everybody. I was among the first who talked to you. Because of your status as a medical person I asked you then, 'Just how serious is the injury?'

"You weren't optimistic. You feared for any sense of normality. In fact, you feared for his life. At the time you looked at his injury scientifically. What's happened since?"

Kathy's eyes shone as she replied, "I can definitely say that I have seen God's supernatural power in bringing Mark back."

"It's been a beautiful sight to behold, hasn't it? I understand that you have been 'specialling' him lately, taking care of him. Tell us about that."

"Well, I spend the week-days with Mark. As he grows in independence, he doesn't need me as much, but I drive him to his physical therapy. I monitor his home therapy and just spend time with him."

"Isn't it wonderful to be part of a family that's had such a real part in his recovery? This body of believers has prayed continuously for him.

"And now you go to Zaire to get involved in medical work, church planting, theological education by extension. You'll work with the Bulgers. And you received a scholarship from Missionary Assistance Program. Do you have all the support you need?"

"I do. My support has been entirely pledged. I also received a fellowship that you mentioned from MAP International. So I am all set financially." Kathy beamed.

"Did you notice the stunned look on their faces when you said all your support is pledged? Isn't that beautiful? Oh, we're so proud of you and thankful!

"Do you think some day you might go to the mission field as a doctor? Have you projected that far into the future?"

"That's a real possibility. I've wanted to be on the mission field for about 20 years…"

Turning to include the congregation, the Pastor prayed, "Father, guide Kathy as she leaves for central Africa…Thanks for the way you have taken care of all her support needs. Thanks for the way you are in the process of healing her brother. Father, we are so grateful."

◆   ◆   ◆

On the days preceding Kathy's departure, she and Mark kept busy. They took time to attend the funeral of our highly respected church administrator who had died suddenly of a heart attack. Even before the service there was standing room only in the main auditorium. Kathy and Mark were forced to climb to the balcony where Bob and I joined them.

We waited until the end of the line to file by the casket. One of the deceased man's daughters, a nurse at a mission hospital in Africa, had flown home to attend her father's funeral. She walked over and embraced Mark and her younger brother reached for Mark's shoulder. Mark looked into the casket, shook hands with the widow, and told her he was sorry for her loss.

Then Pastor said, "Mark, I love you," and embraced our son. Deeply moved, Mark wept aloud in Pastor's arms. After regaining composure he walked to the foyer where he talked with two friends. "No one would have been surprised seeing me in that casket," he said, "but everyone is shocked by Buele's death."

FRIDAY, MARCH 2

This has been a good, full day. How thrilled I was this evening to hear Mark say, "I feel good about myself," after we'd returned from a dinner with some of Kathy's friends.

And then, blessings upon blessings, deaconess, Yvonne Rook, agreed to take Kathy's place as Mark's attendant. Thank You, Lord.

◆   ◆   ◆

Kathy and Mark attended the Match Day at the medical center where students learned their residency placements. Originally our daughter planned to rank schools in the mid-west and farther east as her preferences. But, wanting to be closer to Mark, she had ranked certain Seattle hospitals highest, even though Washington programs rarely accepted Oregon students.

That evening Kathy told us, "In this tense and dramatic moment one of the faculty handed me a sealed envelope. I ripped it open and my jaw dropped. I'll be going to Bethesda Lutheran Medical Center in St. Paul, Minnesota."

Bob and I were stunned. "Kathy, I'm sorry. St. Paul sounds a long way off, but we need to accept this decision as God's will, too," I said, keeping my emotions in check.

SUNDAY, MARCH 25

Today, Kathy departed for Africa. Before leaving she spoke in both morning church services and in our Sunday school class. We rushed home and shared a quiet, somber mealtime, not knowing quite what to say. When Bob loaded Kathy's luggage into the car, Mark cried, but he soon regained his composure.

After arriving at the airport, Mark, with canes, walked steadily to the departure gate where over 50 friends joined us. They prayed and wished Kathy God's blessing.

Mark greeted everyone, too. They were as excited observing Mark's progress as in anticipating Kathy's ministry.

Mark, a great host, restrained his emotions. "But that wasn't how I really felt," he said as we walked back to the car. "It was so hard saying goodbye to Kathy." He choked up.

Even though Bob and I support Kathy's mission project, we also know that she leaves with mixed emotions. As deeply as she desires to support Mark, she also feels called to a medical mission's assignment.

Still, we believe Kathy's departure will aid Mark in his search for independence.

14

Growing Toward Independence

o o o o o o o o o o o o o o o o o o o o o o o o o o o o o o o o o o

God raises the level of the impossible.

—*Corrie Ten Boom*

At Dr. Ward's suggestion we planned a one-hour home conference with a rehab consultant. Bette Nelson, an amiable person, casually asked Mark several questions.

"Mark, tell me about your therapy schedule.

"What rebuilding do you think is needed?

"What are your skills and interests?

"What are your short-and long-range goals?"

Bob and I observed their interactions. Mark responded to each question slowly, at times having difficulty finding the right words to express his thoughts.

"I have a long road ahead of me," he said, "but I want to continue schooling. I'd like to begin seminary training and improve my communication skills," he concluded.

The consultant seemed pleased with her findings and we felt affirmed and encouraged. She recommended that Mark be tested by a rehabilitation psychologist. When we suggested Dr. Paul Sundstrom, a Christian psychologist who had experience in this field, she gave us immediate approval.

The following day, Dr. Sundstrom's receptionist informed me that he was not taking new patients. My heart sank.

"But this is for our son, Mark Laughlin"...

She interrupted. "Wait a second. Maybe he'll take Mark."

Within moments she scheduled an appointment for April 16. In closing the conversation, the receptionist introduced herself and I could hear her smile over the phone. "Mark's a friend of mine," she said.

TUESDAY, MARCH 27

How can I ever doubt Your love, Lord? You daily show me You are at work in our lives. I believe Mark's appointment with Dr. Sundstrom is by divine intervention.

◆   ◆   ◆

The "catastrophic insult" cost Mark his driver's license. Therefore, that Saturday afternoon, Bob drove Mark to a nearby school parking lot where our son practiced basic driving skills. A short time later, while standing at the kitchen sink, I looked up to see Mark grinning from ear-to-ear as he drove the car into the driveway. His wide turn made tread marks on the lawn, but who cared?

"My right foot moved slowly," Mark reported. "Dad drove onto our street and I drove the last two blocks. I did an okay job," he said with eyes sparkling.

SATURDAY, MARCH 31

After a leisurely dinner, some friends, Bob, Mark, and I watched the video of Mark explaining to Duane the relationship between God and man. We were all encouraged by our son's deft way with the teenager except Mark.

"I'll never talk that way again," Mark said sadly. He saw only hurdles to overcome.

I blame myself for not foreseeing this possible outcome. Mark needs time for mending his mind, body, and fear-ridden spirit. Lord, help me to be more aware of his frailty.

◆   ◆   ◆

"It's hard to distinguish what God's perfect will is," Mark penned in his diary. "My reading is only mediocre. My thoughts are simple. My speech is atrocious."

Later that day Mark said, "My physical therapist was angry when I told her I drove my stick-shift. But she had me drive in a vacant parking lot close to RIO. Then she had me drive on surrounding streets and, Mom, the traffic was scary.

But they were satisfied and said I could apply for my driver's license." Mark paused for a moment and said with a sigh, "I was petrified. Driving takes deep concentration."

"I finished a license application describing my bicycle accident and left the form for Dr. Ward's' signature. His secretary will mail it to the DMV [Department of Motor Vehicles] for their 'okay.' "I'll really have to study that manual," Mark said.

"Great progress, Mark. You'll be driving soon," I replied.

SATURDAY, APRIL 7

Mark designed a stencil of musical notes. His aunt helped him silk-screen them. The long, tiring project unraveled Mark and the finished product didn't measure up to his expectations. He felt his efforts were a failure.

Lord, show me more ways to affirm Mark. His self-esteem is so fragile, but may he dwell on the fact that his self-worth comes from You.

MONDAY, APRIL 9.

Mark likes the simple occupational therapy tasks that he has begun at Bob's office: copying, filing, indexing, and entering orders on the computer. But he also feels discouraged because of his slow pace and lack of balance.

TUESDAY, APRIL 10

While waiting for the DMV exam Mark moved downstairs. He worked hours rearranging furniture and hanging posters, giving rapt attention to each detail.

The journey to Mark's room provides exercise. Still, the long distance and stair-climbing exhausts him.

◆   ◆   ◆

Mark celebrated another landmark after moving downstairs. He received permission to sleep without his heavy foot casts on a 10-day trial basis. He had worn these casts nightly for seven months to help prevent contractures of his feet. The cumbersome casts, restricting the movement of his feet, imprisoned him.

"Naked feet in bed. I'm not sure how I'll handle that," Mark said, chuckling. When April 11 finally rolled around Mark took his written driver's test. "I missed three out of 25 questions," he said, triumphantly. Then I helped Mark change from his hiking boots into lighter shoes. With the use of canes Mark trudged to his nearby car. "How long will you be gone," I asked the tester.

"About 20 minutes."

"Will Mark come back into the building?"

"Only if he passes the test."

I thought of Matthew 7:7: "Ask and it will be given to you; seek and you will find; knock and the door will be opened to you." I was confident Mark could pass the test but realized that he must remain calm and not feel threatened by the examiner.

I prayed non-stop for 20 minutes, asking God to help Mark remain relaxed and think clearly. I asked that the tester be considerate and understanding.

Then, to my joy, I heard slow, irregular steps with infrequent tapping of canes. Peering around the corner, I saw him aglow with success. God had answered my petitions.

Mark received 34 out of a possible 38 points. Three points were lost because of the slowness of his right foot. The other point dealt with Mark's inability to readily turn his head to the left.

A clerk in the testing room looked over the final scores of both tests. He turned the sheets over and over, scanning each line.

"Mark, what limitations have been placed on your driving?"

"None."

The clerk examined each section a second time as though he could not believe it.

"I congratulate you," the supervisor said as he came over to shake Mark's hand.

We left the building in silence. Mark stopped and attempted to leap, but neither foot left the ground. He didn't care. He clapped his hands.

"God is so good," Mark said.

WEDNESDAY, APRIL 11

Lord, my heart is still pounding after Mark's victory with the DMV. He no longer needs an attendant to chauffeur him. What a confidence builder.

As Mark drove home he admitted, "I'll dread purchasing gasoline. I'm afraid the attendant won't be able to hear me."

Lord, just a small favor-please strengthen and clarify Mark's speech.

SATURDAY, APRIL 14

With renewed zeal, Mark designed another stencil while I stood by to give him moral support. Mark perspired heavily, his body trembling throughout the long, tedious silk screening job. The end result was worth his creative efforts; he produced lovely musical symbols on stationery.

Mark said, "This'll be a gift for Kathy's graduation."

◆   ◆   ◆

By special invitation, Bob, Mark, and I attended West Hills Christian Church. The pastor preached a lesson about Paul. "Though Paul was in the will of God he was redirected." He then introduced our son. "Mark is a modern-day example of Paul, set aside for unknown purposes." He then asked the believers to pray that Mark would be given the capacity to return to seminary.

Bob, Mark, and I each gave a short testimony. At the conclusion of Mark's words, a little girl came forward to accept Christ. After the service, many of the congregation came to greet Mark and they promised to pray for his complete recovery.

MONDAY, APRIL 16

Mark feels good about his lengthy meeting with Dr. Sundstrom. We anxiously await the results of the aptitude and achievement tests he has taken.

◆ ◆ ◆

Bob and I joined Mark at an appointment with Dr. Markham, his neurosurgeon. "You're one in a hundred. I've never before talked to anyone in an intelligent conversation that has been where you were. You'll be back in school.

"How much pain did you have?"

"I don't remember any."

"What do you remember during your coma?"

"I don't recall a thing."

"Well," Dr. Markham mused, "your recovery amazes me."

"Dr. Markham," I said as we were departing, "Kathy has learned that, as a doctor, there are some things that she might not tell her patients' families."

"Was she critical of me?"

"Oh, no. But she learned that there are some things which may be better left unsaid."

Markham paused a moment and reflected. "It was after I told you those terrible, black things that I walked away and wept."

15

Laugh And Cry With Me

○ ○

Character cannot be developed in ease and quiet. Only through experience of trial and suffering...

—Helen Keller

After his doctor's appointments, Mark, Bob, and I attended a Judson fundraising banquet. To Mark's surprise, the college president asked him to sit at the head table. When introduced, Mark received a standing ovation and was asked to speak. Bob and I were thrilled and overcome, reflecting on how far Mark had progressed.

Mark stood and, without faltering, addressed the group for a few moments. In conclusion he said, "Day by day God continues to bring me back. My desire is to return to seminary. I covet your continued prayers." A swell of emotion stirred throughout the audience of over 300, like the wind of the Spirit.

MONDAY, APRIL 16 (Cont.)

This evening was a thriller for Mark, Bob, and me, Lord, but You know how fragile his emotional control is. Today he overextended himself. It's hard for me to admit, Lord, that Mark is so labile. What will tomorrow hold?

◆   ◆   ◆

Mark stopped by the bank the next morning and broke down when he spoke. As he tried to leave, leaning heavily on his canes, I could see he needed help. Walking outside with Mark, I steadied him by holding onto his belt from the back until he could sit down in his car. We prayed together and I said, "Don't drive, Tiger, until you regain control."

Returning to my desk, I, too, cried and escaped into the supply room. Our keen-eyed receptionist followed me.

"I care that you hurt," she said, putting an arm around me.

"Everyone here's been so supportive," I said, "but no one here has seen me cry before."

"Weep all you want, cuz' I have a shoulder for you to cry on," she replied, hugging me.

FROM MARK'S JOURNAL, TUESDAY, APRIL 17

Yesterday and today were as different as night and day. Yesterday was the sensational one. It started with a meeting with Dr. Sundstrom. He made me feel at home. I had a few tears, but they were quickly gone and things got better.

We then had a meeting with Dr. Markham. He's convinced that I have a great future...just months away.

The day finished with a great dinner at the Columbia [Gorge] Hotel, surrounded by supporters of the Judson concept. They asked me, of all people, to sit at the head table. I was honored to the max. They asked me to speak to the group and tell them of the progress I'd made. It's a good thing I didn't take today's attitude along last night.

I was in an awful mood today. I felt that my progress had ended. I don't feel I will progress to the level I had in the past. God knows, I don't.

◆   ◆   ◆

Later in the week Dr. Sundstrom announced Mark's test results. Beaming, he said, "Most of Mark's former knowledge and recall are intact. He ranks 98th percentile in math, a response triggered from the right side of the brain. He's dropped to the 93rd percentile in language and usage and 84th percentile in spelling, responses triggered from the damaged, left side of the brain."

Bob, Mark, and I listened and smiled.

Sundstrom continued, "In sight, hearing, and movement Mark remains above average, but his ability to learn and store new information remains weak. Mark, also, is slightly below average in time required to complete a task."

"Mark, I encourage you to rebuild these deficient areas by reading and working on language skills, including college and graduate tests.

"You're like an actor on stage who can never step out of character. That's what makes it so hard. The rest of us in the audience can come and go at will.

"Mark, can you express your feelings freely with your family?" Mark thought a moment before responding, "Yes," with quivering lips.

"Good. It's important for you to express yourself freely and release your emotions. That way you'll have a healthy recovery."

Those words were comforting and confirmed we were doing some things right. Mark, too, expressed relief. He needed freedom of expression without guilt.

"Mark, do you resent your mother's help with your passive exercises?"

Mark replied, "No, because I know how much Mom loves me." He put one hand up to his chin as though it would help him maintain composure.

"It would take anyone else two or more years to get where you are, Mark. You're a phenomenon. I'm confident you'll attend seminary in the fall," Sundstrom said ecstatically.

FRIDAY, APRIL 20

Bob, Mark, and I still revel in the prospect that he will be able to reenter seminary. How heartwarming, too, when Mark came into the living room, stretched his arms around me, and said, "I sure love you, Mom." I had feared Mark would never hug me again. Now his embrace ended a perfect day.

◆   ◆   ◆

Kathy could not be contacted by phone in Zaire, but Mark wrote her daily, giving an account of his improvements. Kathy 's frequent letters vividly described the lush, tropical paradise around Rwanguba and painted word pictures about the fascinating nationals. She also wrote, "My heart is with you, Mark, Mom, and Dad. I live for your letters."

SATURDAY, APRIL 21

After Mark's visit to Providence he reported, "I received hugs from many of my caregivers. What an affirming time. I believe someday I'll be normal."

SATURDAY, APRIL 28

Mark now walks with one cane, eight months after his accident.

While Kathy finishes her fellowship in Zaire we are planning her graduation and farewell for June 10. I was thrilled this week that Mark could hand print 250 invitation envelopes for the farewell reception.

After that, we will say goodbye again when she leaves for Bethesda Hospital in Minnesota.

Lord, I'm grateful Mark is becoming more aware of the world outside himself and wants to be part of it. Still, new blessings daily.

MONDAY, MAY 7

In one of his down moods Mark attended our Bible study. When a member asked him about his feelings, Mark replied, "I'm not angry with God but I'm afraid-afraid of what the future holds for me."

I wonder, too, what the future holds for Mark. Lord, how can I help Mark, besides reminding him that You said, "Do not be afraid?"

MONDAY, MAY 14

I enrolled Mark in an exercise swimming class but he couldn't do any of the basic water exercises. The traumatic swimming experience left Mark weeping.

"I'm not normal. I feel retarded because I can't swim now."

Did we run ahead of You, Lord? What else can we do?

◆   ◆   ◆

One evening I placed an old family picture on the piano. Mark looked at it and then mused, "That's what I used to be like. I need a friend who cares. I mean, other than you, Dad, and Kathy."

"Of course," I responded. "Someone your own age to have fun and fellowship with."

"It's painful now. I miss Anne, but I want to move on to other friends, guys and gals. If my life is ever to be like others, I need them."

WEDNESDAY, MAY 23

Mark reluctantly allowed me to check his aphasia workbook, which helped him to retrieve correct words, an ability he needed to strengthen. When he missed a question he said, "I was trying to be creative." Was he being funny or having trouble admitting he checked the wrong answer?

But, thanks, Lord, Mark is doing well and making fewer mistakes.

FROM MARK'S JOURNAL, SATURDAY, MAY 26

I worked harder than I have in a long time [helping Dad paint the deck] and had an interesting emotional response. I was tuckered-I erupted in tears for no apparent reason-This action surprised, and disappointed me. I have to learn not to exhaust myself, because the physical is very closely linked to the emotional.

◆   ◆   ◆

When we talked about Kathy's return from Zaire, Mark wept again.

"It's selfish of me, but Kathy will be coming home to her graduation and to all that fun and celebration. It makes my angry that I can't even talk and walk."

For an hour Mark unleashed pent-up feelings, then apologized. Dr. Sundstrom told us, however, that his periodic wallow in self-pity was an important part of his grief and loss therapy.

Mark recovered his composure then suggested that we surprise Kathy in Seattle the following day when she expected to transfer to another plane. What a great idea.

TUESDAY, MAY 29

Kathy called this afternoon to tell us of her ninety-minute delay in her New York departure. She would likely miss her Seattle connection. We were so excited about surprising her in Seattle that I didn't reveal our plan. If I am being a little deceptive, Lord, please forgive me.

◆   ◆   ◆

Mark drove most of the way to Seattle. Bob and I decided he should greet Kathy before we appeared on the scene.

When Mark broke into a grin, we knew he had spotted his sister. Kathy ran toward Mark and they wrapped themselves in each other's arms. Finally, Bob and I shouted, "Surprise." We laughed and hugged. For a moment, our world stood still.

On the way home, Mark and Kathy chatted for an hour. Mark talked freely and with animation; he'd never seemed happier. He then drove while Bob slept. When we arrived at 2:00 a.m. Bob and I went to bed, but Kathy and Mark continued talking.

The next morning we realized that Mark had again over-extended himself.

FROM MARK'S JOURNAL, WEDNESDAY, MAY 30

I had a rather discouraging day based solely on my actions with Kathy. I love her dearly. She's very special. But she's also very intelligent, so smart that she makes me feel bad in comparison. She'll graduate in June with a medical degree, while I'll celebrate an anniversary in August related to a terrible accident. In some ways that makes me feel left out when many people are celebrating.

But my pessimism is slanted. I'm slowly making progress. It would be beneficial to gaze on the optimistic side. There will always be someone eager to look on the negative side. I want to be unique. I really want to boggle a few people with my good nature and well-adjusted mind-set. By myself I can do nothing, but with God and a positive attitude I can make progress.

FROM MARK'S JOURNAL, MONDAY, JUNE 4

Kathy confessed to me that she's struggling with opposite emotions. She rejoices over her upcoming graduation and sorrows over the continued financial difficulties at the bank [of which Dad had been the chief organizer]. Mom and Dad do a great job of hiding their disappointment, but deep pain is there.

◆   ◆   ◆

Kathy's anticipated graduation, called hooding day, had arrived. Her special friend, Steve Classen, joined us. Kathy graduated Magna cum Laude, receiving two awards. Then the highest honor was announced.

"The Edward S. Hayes Gold-headed Cane Award, with the trust it symbolizes," began the professor, "has been presented yearly since 1967 to a member of the graduating class who has been selected for this high honor by a vote of his or her peers and teachers. The honor is presented to the person they perceive has the most qualities they desire in their own physician, to the student who demonstrates compassion, devotion, and effective service to the sick. It is presented with the conviction that they will forever epitomize and uphold the traditions of the True Physician.

"This year's honor goes to Dr. Kathleen Marie Laughlin."

Her peers and the faculty sprang to their feet, applauding wildly, joined by the audience.

Kathy walked up to the podium and quietly said, "Thank you."

Obviously moved, she stood for a moment, head bowed, and then began, "I think this is the highest honor I've ever received. There are so many I'd like to thank.

I'd like to thank teachers and professors who have encouraged and prodded us through these last four years.

"I'd also like to thank my father, mother, and brother for their constant and total support. They have been excellent examples of love, hope, and determination.

"And I'd also like to thank God who gives me strength and purpose. Medical school is truly a shared experience. Because we've struggled, supported, talked, laughed, and even cried together, this award belongs to each of you. Thank you."

In the midst of her deepest turmoil, Kathy questioned God. But her recent comments at church and her acceptance statement made me realize she had won a spiritual victory.

WEDNESDAY, JUNE 6

As Kathy was honored gratitude swept over Bob, Mark, and me. However, my deepest joy was watching Mark. He proudly smiled while leaning heavily on his canes. That he could even be in the audience, sharing in this milestone moment of his sister's life overwhelmed me. She had known, only too well, the reasons for those black medical predictions regarding Mark's likely dependencies. But her compassion, encouragement, and well-trained skills had helped pull him through. I praise You, Lord.

THURSDAY, JUNE 7

It appeared at noon that our dreams of supporting Christian ministries through Stewardship Bank might come true. But needed capital could not be raised. The bank was closed by FDIC at 6:00 p.m. Why our dreams and hopes had been snuffed out I did not know. Even the management team of three bank officers, with a total of 72 years experience, hadn't helped.

You know, Lord, how Bob and I have struggled with this crisis. Now the poised hammer's blow struck hard. Both Bob and I wept but brought our emotions under control, determined not to mar Kathy's graduation.

How can we handle such contrasts, Lord, the death of a promising concept and the joyful fulfillment of Kathy's dream of becoming a medical doctor? Only You, Lord, have the answer.

FROM MARK'S JOURNAL, THURSDAY, JUNE 7

Graduation was the biggest event of the day, big, but not necessarily exciting, but my walk was a highlight. I walked almost three blocks faltering only once. But I was pleased with the longest distance I've walked yet. Exciting!

SUNDAY, JUNE 10

Our home was a beehive this afternoon for Kathy's farewell. At times the entry hall, living-dining area, and deck were flooded with well-wishers, and others stood outside waiting to come in. Many sensed our hidden grief and quietly extended their condolences regarding the bank closure.

Kathy was joyful. Mark beamed as everyone talked with him. Guests drained the punch bowl and ate the 60 dozen cookies Mark and I had baked.

We thank You for orchestrating all the details so perfectly, Lord.

FRIDAY, JUNE 15

Kathy invited us to help her set up house in St. Paul, Minnesota. For a week we prepared for the two-car trip. She packed and shipped her household items.

Lord, please guard us as we travel. Direct Kathy's shipment so that it will be delivered the same day we arrive in the Twin Cities.

TUESDAY, JUNE 19

Fun and stresses filled our four-day journey. We traded off driving and also exchanging traveling partners, but Mark usually traveled with Kathy.

The afternoon before our anticipated arrival we became slaphappy. In the car ahead, Mark held a large sign out the window: "HELP! OUT OF GAS!"

Such nonsense helped us relax. We were actually having fun.

Thank You, Lord, for allowing us to be ourselves again.

WEDNESDAY, JUNE 20

Arriving in St. Paul, we drove to Kathy's apartment in the hospital complex.

Bob carried boxes in and Mark helped unpack and set up the stereo. He hung pictures and framed some of his own photographic efforts.

FROM MARK'S JOURNAL, SUNDAY, JUNE 24

This is destined to be a tough day. Birthdays are supposed to be celebrations, joyous events commemorating another year of progress toward the ultimate goal God has destined for you.

Somehow I feel different this morning. If God envisioned my advancement, why did He slow my walking? If God wanted me to communicate His love toward others, why did He make my speech so difficult?

Somehow I thought God had plans for my perfect progress. But it turns out he has perfect plans for my progress. Is it only coincidental that half of the letters in the word "patience" spell the word "pain?" I suppose you can't possess the former until you learn how to deal with the latter. But it's so hard!

Why doesn't God give you pain when you're amply equipped with patience? It would be much easier then. Perhaps God is illustrating how closely linked the two are; if you had no pain, what need would there be for patience?

God, I think, is giving me a big lesson in both. The pain is lessening daily. The patience is slowly, but surely, making progress. I need to be very sensitive to the reality of both, cautious of their effect on my life, but ready to face the pain with patience.

◆   ◆   ◆

Kathy ably summed up our thoughts in a note on Mark's birthday card: We're another year older and wiser. Sometimes I just feel older. But I think the wisdom is slowly being developed.

Solomon says an interesting thing about wisdom that reminds me of what you said about patience. In Ecclesiastes 1:18 (NASB) he says, "in much wisdom there is much grief." It seems suffering must precede wisdom.

He also says "There is an appointed time for everything…

"A time to tear down, and a time to build up.

"A time to weep, and a time to laugh;

"A time to mourn, and a time to dance" (Eccl. 3:1-4, NASB). Your turn to dance is coming, Happy birthday and happy year.

◆   ◆   ◆

We departed early from St. Paul and struggled with tears and the strain of parting. We followed Kathy on the freeway until she turned off to the university. Mark rolled down the window and waved. Kathy was still waving as we lost sight of her.

"I'm embarrassed about my emotions," Mark said. "Still, it would be worse if we weren't able to express ourselves."

THURSDAY, JUNE 28

We phoned Kathy when we arrived home. She likes her position and co-workers, but said, "I'm lonely in the evenings. I've always been sought out and now I need to reach out. I need others."

◆   ◆   ◆

For the first time since the accident Mark walked at church without canes. People who knew him smiled, knowing what a triumph this was. That evening, after the service, our deaconesses held a farewell reception for Pastor and his wife, serving over 1,000 guests. After 10 years of an effective, faithful ministry, they felt called to an out-of-town church.

Mark wanted to tell them goodbye, but felt he could not risk the potential embarrassment of an emotional outburst. Instead he sat in the car, reading a book.

MONDAY, JULY 9

With Mark's knowledge and involvement the plans for August 11 are progressing well. Some special college classmates will help us celebrate Mark's first anniversary since his surgery as well as the 18th anniversary of the day he accepted Christ as his personal savior.

Lord, may this celebration honor You and make Mark happy.

SATURDAY, AUGUST 11

Shortly after noon, I asked Mark to answer the doorbell.

"Happy birthday, Mark." Kathy flung her arms around him.

"I'm so happy! I'm so happy!" Mark repeated in a high-pitched tone, ecstatic that Kathy had flown home.

The fellowship of family and friends made a perfect day.

FROM MARK'S JOURNAL, SATURDAY, AUGUST 11

Did my sister's surprise visit excite me? I'll answer that by admitting that my voice was far from normal for about a half hour. Kathy's return was a joyful time for me, a time when I was able to carry on the best conversation I'd been capable of for a long time. That was encouraging!

16

Rebuilding

○ ○

Patience is the art of hoping.

—*Vauvenargues*

MONDAY, AUGUST 13

Dr. Ward is very pleased with Mark's progress but suggested that his vocal chords be checked. He also advised Mark to talk with the throat specialist about cosmetic surgery on his trach scar.

What more could we have asked for, Lord? We give You praise.

WEDNESDAY, AUGUST 15

For the first time since the accident, Mark cycled a short distance while Bob jogged alongside. "When I turned, I would've fallen if Dad hadn't been there."

Although Mark's performance fell short of his expectations, he called Kathy reporting his accomplishment.

◆   ◆   ◆

Because Mark required less concentration for completing tasks, simple functions became more normal. Blow-drying his hair had seemed complicated. He had to plug in the cord. Turn on the switch. Direct hot air toward his hair. Now these tasks became more spontaneous. Also, he could claim victory by putting his contacts in after weeks of unsuccessful attempts. When Mark discovered the major problem he was embarrassed. He had been putting his right contact into his left eye.

FRIDAY, AUGUST 17

I'm glad to see Mark's progress in language development with Susan's help. He amazes me with his appetite for leisure reading. Not only has he completed several workbooks, including another one on aphasia, but he has taken graduate record exams and college scholastic tests. Yet, when he falls short of his expectation, he is devastated and still weeps.

Lord, I'm like a leaf in a storm, and Mark's tears are the wind.

◆   ◆   ◆

Mark's physical therapist assigned him additional exercises and he now had 37 daily routines. Mark appeared to have normal balance from side to side, but lacked balance backward and forward causing him to be painstakingly careful of his mindful walk.

We were told, however, that the brain could do some retraining. Possibly the signal sequence to the right thigh muscle could be corrected and his walk become less mechanical.

WEDNESDAY, AUGUST 22

Such great news. The throat specialist said Mark's palate and vocal cords function within the normal range. But he has referred Mark to a speech clinic for a second opinion.

MONDAY, AUGUST 27

The clinic's findings confirm the throat specialist's report. Mark no longer has a paralyzed soft palate. His vocal cords are normal. Thanks to one year's patient, daily inhalation exercises on the spirometer, Mark's voice, though soft, continues to improve. He'll receive additional speech therapy to build volume and clarity.

We thank You that Mark does not need a palate lift or surgery.

TUESDAY, AUGUST 28

Our church college intern asked Mark to consider co-leading a Bible study. Mark's both excited and terrified and I have fears, too.

Mark called Dave Wahlstrom and discussed with him the possibility of assisting with the Bible study. "I need to get out and see how much of me is really left," I overheard Mark say.

Mark's wisdom left me breathless.

◆　　　◆　　　◆

At our condo at the coast, Mark and I attempted a two-mile walk on the beach in spite of the fog. After an hour, his pace slowed and sense of balance lessened. He stopped, held on to me for support, and struggled for balance. "My brain refuses to cooperate. It gives out and says, 'No,'" Mark lamented.

Then dense fog engulfed us and our destination disappeared. Still, Mark remained determined. We walked a few feet, stopped, and prayed. We started walking again, then prayed again. Finally the condominium came into view. This spurred Mark on and we soon saw a worried Bob walking toward us.

The tiresome journey took over two hours and left Mark exhausted, but triumphant.

SUNDAY, SEPTEMBER 2

Lord, I'm still working through forgiving those who erred in Mark's pre-hospital care. You know how difficult this part of my grief recovery is.

I know from Your Word that forgiving is an act of obedience, a decision, an act of my will. I'm finding, too, that forgiving happens gradually—I'm canceling the debt.

Forgiving is not forgetting, acquittal, excusing, or reconciliation. But by Your power, Lord, I'm no longer controlled, or obsessed, by the need to continually recall the situation. I'm observing slow, continual progress on my road to recovery and am being set free. Thank You.

◆　　　◆　　　◆

Mark had spent weeks planning, ordering, and then building a darkroom for his photography projects. Then came the day when he printed, matted, and framed numerous scenic photo groupings for wedding gifts. His talent showed through in the creative results.

TUESDAY, SEPTEMBER 4

This is becoming a habit, Lord. Mark has over-extended himself physically again. As a result, his fragile emotional balance can't handle the pressure and his photographic projects frustrated him.

Candidly, Mark told me, "I feel cheated. I'm number two and Kathy is number one. Maybe I'm jealous of her because she's excelling while I'm struggling."

Lord, I could listen to this calmly, glad that Mark didn't try to stuff his feelings. This road is familiar territory, but we are going this route less often. The ruts aren't as deep and the path isn't as long. Mark feels better when the journey ends, but then wonders why he put us through such pain.

WEDNESDAY, SEPTEMBER 5

This is a momentous day, Lord. Mark registered to audit one seminary class and also decided he'll co-lead the Bible study group. May he honor You and may You bless his efforts.

◆   ◆   ◆

Bob and Mark attended the annual CBA Men's Round-Up at Camp Tadmor near Lebanon, Oregon. Bob was excited about attending his 28th consecutive Round-Up, and Mark saw his attendance as evidence of his recovery. His only concession was to take a cane because of the rough terrain.

Upon their return Bob reported, "We were asked to be part of the Saturday evening program. Mark climbed the stairs to the platform slowly. He had one hand on his cane and the other on my shoulder.

"The 1,800 men sang, 'How Great Thou Art.' I gave a progress report and then thanked the men for praying for Mark during the past year.

"When Mark approached the podium, the men applauded. He broke into tears. The crowd gave him a standing ovation. The song leader came forward and led the men in 'God is so Good.'

"The song leader told Mark he'd made his point. But Mark said he wanted to speak.' He thanked them for praying and said God has answered and then asked them to pray for his continued recovery. He requested they pray as he audited a seminary course and that he'd have the ability to prepare for missions.

"Twenty-five men came forward at the end of the evening's program. Five of the men made decisions for Christ," Bob concluded, visibly moved by the results.

TUESDAY, SEPTEMBER 18

Round-Up participants from three different churches stated that Mark's testimony was the highlight of the weekend. Each called to say they had reported on the event in their Sunday evening church services. "He touched many hearts," one gentleman said.

Thank You, Lord. What seemed to be a tragedy is turning out to be a miracle.

SATURDAY, SEPTEMBER 22

Before the accident Mark participated in several weddings by singing or serving as a groomsman. In two upcoming weddings Mark felt he wasn't asked to participate because of his physical limitations. The thought tormented him.

In one case the bridegroom backed away from Mark as if he didn't exist. Our son was invited to the ceremony but the reception invitation was crossed out with ink.

"It hurts when you are separated from the norm," Mark said, staring at the communication in disbelief. "Help me to forgive him, Lord," Mark added. "What was his purpose? How could he have been so cruel?"

Yet, the other friend was sensitive to Mark's needs. Bob, Mark, and I arrived at the church moments before the ceremony started. The thoughtful groom was still waiting at the door to give Mark a hug before he quickly joined the wedding party.

Lord, that hug made Mark's day and mine, too.

◆   ◆   ◆

Mark finally had cosmetic surgery on his neck to remove the trach scar tissue. The surgeon cut an elongated piece of flesh from Mark's neck. He snipped and stretched the muscles and skin. By evening a wide black and blue band developed around the front of Mark's neck and extended into his chest. Fortunately, he didn't feel as bad as he looked. I was concerned about the extensive bruising, but a call to Kathy put my heart at ease.

SUNDAY, OCTOBER 7

Mark was overjoyed when Dave Wahlstrom and his fiancé, Katy, asked him to be the first groomsman in their wedding.

Mark feels honored and is still smiling. My heart overflows, too.

◆   ◆   ◆

The work demanded by Mark's seminary class overwhelmed him. Although intimidated by the volume of note taking and assignments required, he applied himself. He discovered that, when he worked earlier in the day, he didn't tire as readily and accomplished more. At the same time, Mark struck out at others because of anger at himself for not being able to do what he used to do without effort. Yet, his anger flashed like lightning and then was gone.

THURSDAY, OCTOBER 18

Mark studied and studied for the mid-term in spite of his short concentration span.

Mark went to the exam hopeful of completing it in class but, instead, brought the test home after glancing over it. He realized he'd not mastered some concepts.

Although only auditing, Mark had hoped to have better memory retention. Lord, we are both disappointed, but help me to affirm Mark in all other areas of his progress.

TUESDAY, NOVEMBER 27

Mark had spent hours researching in the library and completing all assignments, including two term papers. The content of the two graduate projects pleased Bob and me. When Mark picked up the graded assignments today the "A's" on both papers confirmed his quality work.

Lord, we rejoice in Your goodness and thank You that Mark's labors have been rewarded.

"But these projects don't match my earlier work," Mark said.

Lord, help Mark to concentrate on his self-worth in You.

◆   ◆   ◆

A rural church pastor had asked our son to give his testimony at their Sunday morning service. In his closing remarks Mark quoted Romans 12:12: "Be joyful in hope, patient in affliction, faithful in prayer.' I'm going through an affliction and need more patience. I still have the desire, and hope to receive training, to serve the Lord. The question is, 'Will I have the ability?'...Will you be faithful in praying that my desire to serve Him will be realized?"

Mark's calmness amazed us. Our son was well organized, spoke from a simple outline, was concise, and felt good about his comments. We sensed that he had touched hearts that morning when a young boy introduced himself after the service ended. "I was given a gold-cross pin for memorizing the books of the Bible," he said. Tears sparkled in his eyes. "I want you to have it. Our class has prayed for you every Sunday since your accident," he added.

At the potluck that followed, many people assured Mark that he spoke clearly and loudly enough for individuals with hearing impairments. Members of the Junior Sunday school Class clustered around Mark all talking at once to their "hero."

THURSDAY, DECEMBER 20

The joy of being a part of Dave's wedding has never worn off. Mark has daily practiced walking up and down steps with someone at his side. Our son made a dashing, dapper groomsman this evening. Guests requested, and waited, for him to escort them. I glowed with thankfulness that Mark again had the privilege of participating in a wedding.

TUESDAY, DECEMBER 25

Kathy flew home for the holidays. The Tidswells were our yearly Christmas dinner guests again. It was like old times, as if Mark's accident had never happened. We had a relaxed time of fun, food, and close fellowship.

After the Tidswells left, at Mark's suggestion, we loaded our gifts into the car, and headed for the coast.

By a midnight fire we opened our presents. Mark's Christmas card had a profound meaning for all of us: "Too often we overlook our greatest gift from God during the holiday time: the simple expression, through His Son's birth, of infinite love. I hope that your thoughts about this blessing will be a great comfort to you during this holiday season."

WEDNESDAY, DECEMBER 26

Kathy and Mark ventured to the swimming pool early this evening. Again, Mark wept because the right leg wouldn't function. Lord, You know I couldn't console him. "I want to be allowed to have some self-pity. God has stripped me and I feel cheated. "I can't cycle. I can't jog. I can't swim. I can't play tennis. Why?" Why? Lord, why? I still wonder, too.

SUNDAY, DECEMBER 30

We returned from the coast and handled Kathy's departure for St. Paul with fewer tears and less stress. Mark, however, still broods over his inability to swim and feels apprehensive about the next seminary class he plans to audit.

Lord, I've seen You best when it was the darkest. Don't let my faith waver now.

TUESDAY, JANUARY 1

Last night the Deaconesses were in charge of refreshments after the New Year's evening service. The college group went ice skating and Mark chose to stay home.

As I walked into our home at 1:30 a.m., I was surprised to hear, "Happy New Year, Mom." I embraced him. "I believe God will continue your healing during this year. Now, Tiger, you'd better get some sleep."

17

Meeting The Challenges

Mercy is unmerited favor from God himself to an erring people who can do nothing to earn it except to hold out their hands.

—Sherwood Wirt

Auditing a seminary class winter term was Mark's main task. He had been assigned a 20-page term paper that, as a whole, overwhelmed him. But one section at a time didn't appear so insurmountable.

SUNDAY, JANUARY 6

I thank You, Lord, for Mark's progress and I ask for further gains. At the same time, when Mark hurts, I hurt, and when Mark cries, I cry. My plea for him is a successful term in seminary.

WEDNESDAY, JANUARY 9

Oh, how Mark is laboring over his course. This afternoon after struggling with those new concepts, in despair he said, "I won't take a class spring term." Lord, I could only smile and say, "We'll accept, Mark, whatever you can handle." But I'm so pained for him. You know my constant plea.

◆   ◆   ◆

While eating breakfast in our sun-filled nook, Mark read from a syndicated newspaper column. "Seventy percent of all parents polled indicated if they had the choice again, they wouldn't have children. How do you feel about that, Mom?"

"The past 17 months have been painful. But I still would have had both you and Kathy.

"I recently read about a child who was killed in an accident," I continued. "The article was written by the victim's father. The child's death wasn't wasted. They grieved his loss, but they knew he was in God's presence. God taught them many things," I added.

"Maybe it would have been better if I'd died, too," Mark said. "You may feel that way now," I replied. "Still, you're improving." Visibly shaken, Mark cradled his head on his arms resting on the table. I continued, "Before you were even conceived you were given to God. I believe He allowed this accident. Because of this experience I believe you'll have a greater ministry.

"Mark, I don't always understand God's purposes, but He took us seriously when your Dad and I made our commitment. I believe you're handling your suffering well. Even through your pain I see God at work."

TUESDAY, FEBRUARY 12

Mark has been poring over Psalm 15, the text for his term project. Part of the assignment was to present his paper orally.

Bob and I gathered in the living room this evening to hear him. Although Mark was tense and fearful, he spoke distinctly, methodically, and expressed concepts well. We couldn't stop praising him for a superb job.

How grateful we are, Lord, for Mark's obvious returning abilities.

FRIDAY, FEBRUARY 22

Mark received 39 out of 40 points on his term project. The professor, Dr. Laney, wrote in positive comments throughout the text.

MONDAY, FEBRUARY 25

Lord, my heart is rejoicing because Mark has signed up to audit another course spring term. And I praise You for his excellent papers.

MONDAY, MARCH 4

Co-leading the Bible study has provided a positive outlet for Mark. I'm pleased the young men are faithful in their attendance.

I thank You, Lord, too, that the experience has built relationships and strengthened Mark's confidence and new learning skills.

◆   ◆   ◆

When the weather warmed, Mark walked with more ease. One morning he decided to mow the front lawn. He strained and struggled, pushing the mower over the lawn several times. Then he turned off the buzzing motor and slowly plodded into the house.

"Mom, I resent that I can't walk. My feet turn out. I walk on the side of my shoes. I have no control. Why has God allowed so much to be taken from me? Is this bitterness?"

After we cried together I said, "Mark, maybe this is bitterness, but I believe that coming to grips with your limitations is part of your coping and healing."

My comment seemed to comfort Mark.

One evening, while completing his exercises, excruciating pain developed in Mark's right side. Fearful of a complication from his accident, I rushed him to Providence's ER. At 1:00 a.m. they wheeled Mark into the operating room and performed an appendectomy.

THURSDAY, MARCH 28

Mark is up and walking this morning after surgery. When the news of Mark's operation reached the rehabilitation unit, several of the hospital staff visited him. He was so pleased. Each visitor was excited to see Mark and complimented him for his drive and progress.

Thanks Lord, for the special attention Mark is receiving.

WEDNESDAY, MAY 1

Mark bounced back so rapidly from surgery that he missed only one class. His unbalanced, impaired walking, however, took a setback and he has less energy.

THURSDAY, MAY 2

Mark completed all the work for his spring term class except for the "walk project" that required a house-to-house survey. Mark didn't feel up to the extended, laborious, mindful walk on uneven ground, and up and down stairs. Even so he, again, received "A's" on his papers.

◆   ◆   ◆

Mark's 18-speed bicycle was stolen from our garage. Fortunately, we had insurance that meant Mark could purchase a similar model. Riding it was another challenge for him. Each attempt to raise his leg over the seat was difficult and sometimes he lost his balance. At first Bob ran alongside, steadying Mark. Later, Mark rode successfully by himself.

MONDAY, JUNE 3

Mark occasionally rides his bike for about 30 minutes. The first time he took a tumble he came home discouraged. Today, even though he scraped his left arm from the wrist to the elbow, he displayed an overcomer's attitude.

"I'm determined to improve with practice," he said.

◆   ◆   ◆

To Mark's surprise, the Providence rehab therapy staff asked him to counsel a 23 year-old head trauma patient. Mark consented, feeling good about being a helpful listener and grateful for the family's appreciation of his counsel. After the second session, the parents invited Mark to dinner. Although drained at the close of the evening, he knew he had encouraged them. Mark also recognized that the young man's greatest problem was controlling his emotions. How well he knew the feeling! Those encounters made Mark realize how far he had progressed.

TUESDAY, JULY 9

Mark had purchased a personal computer in early May. He has taken to his toy like a duck to water even though he just confessed that he bought the computer believing he'd prove to Bob and me that he wasn't recovering as we claimed.

Lord, You're shining through Mark.

◆   ◆   ◆

Our family visited our former Pastor and his wife, now ministering at the Evangelical Free Church in Rockford, IL. They embraced us in a heart-warming reunion before ushering us to our reserved seats. During the welcome to visitors Pastor introduced us. He then said, "Mark, remain standing. I want the congregation to view a miracle." Pastor gave a brief history about Mark saying that he was a modern-day phenomenon, the greatest miracle Pastor and his wife had seen in their 34 years of ministry.

At lunch Pastor asked Mark if he felt bitter about his accident. As we listened intently, Mark replied, "I don't think I'm bitter. I have concerns and am bewildered, but I still have a desire to serve God."

"I wish our congregation could hear your voice. They need to hear what you're saying.

"Mark, I see you ministering on a one-to-one basis or in small groups. You've earned the right to be heard. You have a platform from which to speak," Pastor concluded.

His counsel and obvious interest encouraged all of us.

Every moment of our stay with Pastor and his wife was filled with sharing, caring, and supporting.

◆   ◆   ◆

Sunday we heard a message on healing. We raised our hands, requesting prayer for healing, and took communion at the altar rail.

After the service Mark asked, "God doesn't seem to be healing me. Is it because of my lack of faith?"

"Mark, it's not instantaneous, but God is healing you," I said.

"It's not because you lack faith. The process is slow, but He is in control," Kathy added.

TUESDAY, SEPTEMBER 3

Home again. Mark faced his next giant hurdle today. Emotionally frayed and fearful, he started his fall term seminary classes for credit.

◆   ◆   ◆

Memory work composed the first section of Mark's Hermeneutics course. Because of his slight aphasia, difficulty remembering proper names (anomia), and trouble learning new concepts, he spent hours condensing lecture notes, defining terms, and listing new vocabulary words and names. General concepts he understood, but new facts didn't come quickly.

I drilled Mark by the hour and we hurt as he struggled to remember. He could state the page and line number and the beginning letter of the word or concept, but couldn't retrieve the total content. He studied hours each day for the first test.

MONDAY, SEPTEMBER 23

Today Mark became distressed. "What do you want from me, God? I want to serve You. The desire is there, but will I have the ability? Why have You made it so hard for me to learn?"

Mark and I sat in silence for a long time.

WEDNESDAY, OCTOBER 2

Another bummer. Mark reported that a professor asked him when he would get rid of his limp.

Mark said he was stunned. He hesitated and then said, "I don't know. It's a gift I've been given."

"Mark, I'm sure he meant well," I responded.

"Sure, but he'll never know how painful his question was," Mark replied.

I was pleased that, because Mark was majoring in counseling, he was required to go through 20 hours of personal counseling. He admitted these sessions had helped him accept his disabilities.

◆   ◆   ◆

Because Mark struggled so hard and long with his studies, my emotions unraveled easily. I entertained fears regarding Mark's entry into seminary.

But that afternoon Mark told me that his Hermeneutics professor called him a miracle and was pleased with his test.

"I told him that a 'C-' didn't match the scholastic performance of the Mark Laughlin I'd known before the accident. I felt like a half-miracle."

Mark had retained what he had studied, but had not studied enough subject matter. Even so, the good news made my day. I praised God for another hurdle crossed.

Mark, on the other hand wept, and said, "I wish I could change my name. I can't meet the Laughlin tradition. I can't learn like the rest anymore. You should have Tim [a musically gifted friend from church] for a son. He is so talented and capable."

"Mark, I wouldn't take 20 Tim's for you. God hasn't forgotten that we gave you back to Him before you were ever conceived. He still has a plan for you," I replied.

The second Hermeneutics test was also preceded by traumatic, repetitive study. Analytically, Mark soon knew where to locate the answer, the exact page, and line. By association, he devised letter symbols that became his personal code for translating into proper names, terms, vocabulary words, or concepts.

The more Mark reviewed his notes, the more he retrieved. His slow, but obvious, progress pleased him, especially when his grade for the second test improved to a "B-."

Mark completed a total of nine personal perception and research papers spending endless hours researching and writing each one. He also shared one term project with two other classmates in a counseling course that concluded with a class presentation.

A typical Mom, I felt irritated that Mark was doing the majority of the work, but he countered, "Studying for 'Coping With the Loss of Health,' Mom, has taught me so much. Mourning is inevitable, and grieving is part of the process. I realize that lamenting the loss, anger, and self-blame need to be dealt with."

Mark could see himself in the case study of an active young person prematurely and permanently deprived physically. Now, he could accept that painful healing takes time, time that may be measured in years.

Mark experienced less turmoil studying for the final in his counseling class. He was pleased with his last test and the completion of his first term. Elatedly, he penned Kathy a note:

> I have called Mom since The Test, but other than her, you're the first to hear. Your brother is going to get married! Kathy? Are you still with us, Doc? Sorry, I was just doing that to make sure you were still awake. I finished my counseling final about a half-hour ago and, let me assure you, I'm excited. Your brother did a good job...I've never left a test feeling such euphoria!
>
> I have one more class to attend...and a final paper to turn in...and then it's VACATION TIME! On a scale from 1 to 10, how excited do you think I am? Good question...I'm not sure that numbers go that high.
>
> Thanks much, Kathy, for your prayers.... I'm glad we'll soon have a week to spend with each other. I'll pray about your closing days in the Twin Cities before your vacation. Lookin' forward to ya'.

MONDAY, DECEMBER 9

Mark received A's on alll three of the semester papers. As we rejoiced, Psalm 116:1,2 came to mind: "I love the Lord, for he heard my voice; he heard my cry for mercy. Because he turned his ear to me, I will call on him as long as I live."

MONDAY, JUNE 2

Lord, it's been months since I've written in my journal. Though spring semester hadn't been as stressful, Mark welcomes the summer break.

Kathy's friendship with Steve Classen has deepened over several years into love. After their May engagement, Steve visited us asking for Bob's, Mark's, and my blessing on their wedding.

"I'll be marrying my best friend. I love her very much," he said. Lord, we thank You for Steve. We love him as our son and brother.

◆   ◆   ◆

We plunged into planning the December wedding, following Kathy's detailed instructions from St. Paul. Amidst the blizzard of her requests, I managed to find time to construct a surprise memory bedspread as a gift. On his computer, Mark organized letters to Kathy and Steve's friends, asking for "memory squares" that would be stitched together. He sketched the design ideas we contributed to the bedspread. Mark surprised us by contributing his own original patterns and embroidery. The summer flew by and soon fall studies absorbed him.

SATURDAY, DECEMBER 27

For months we've prayed for good weather for Kathy's wedding. It's just like You, God, to provide a balmy, crystal-bright day.

Kathy's dream of a Christmas celebration became a reality before a chapel full of happy guests. Beyond that it was her unspeakable joy to have Mark as one of their groomsmen.

Before Steve and Kathy left the reception, Steve hugged me. "Now I guess I can call you Mom," he said. I rejoiced because we were gaining a great son-in-law. He will treat Kathy well. I can't imagine a better match.

I'm excited for another development in Mark's life, also. During the extended, extra-busy holiday season, You, Lord, strengthened his emotions. He's ready to tackle seminary classes again.

◆   ◆   ◆

Many of our friends continued to pray for Mark daily. They are taking part in God's plan to bring triumph out of tragedy. Bob and I had changed, too.

Our dependency on the Lord had deepened. We'd become more keenly aware that not all scars are visible to the naked eye. That forgiveness was a gift you gave yourself and that faith was realizing that we were useful to God not in spite of our scars but because of them. Therefore, our sensitivity to others' emotional, mental, physical, and spiritual needs had heightened. Our ministry opportunities had increased because we were better equipped to support others in crisis. We more keenly recognized the importance of prayer. We had learned that, though we couldn't trust our feelings, God is always trustworthy.

◆   ◆   ◆

We asked friends to reflect on what Mark's accident had meant to them.

One friend of Mark's responded, "My thoughts after watching you two cope with the probable loss of Mark during the surgery that night were ones of admiration and respect. I was watching a family being 'tried in the fire.' There were only words of trust in and commitment to God. I have praised God often as you have gone through such trying times."

One dear friend, since deceased, left a loving legacy when she wrote, "The testimony of God's people had an affect on all the medical and nursing staff and your family's transparency-hurts, pains, and joys-blessed others."

A staff member at our church contributed this candid opinion: "I viewed Bob and Milli's optimism about Mark's recovery as admirable but perhaps not 'realistic.' I believed that God could and probably would heal him, but the 'what ifs' came to mind...He might choose a future for Mark which I wouldn't be able to understand."

My angel nurse gave us an amazing tribute:"I remember watching Bob, who is frequently teased as being an 'eternal optimist,' show an undying faith that kept us all going and looking for the rainbow in the clouds.

"I remember watching Milli let God be the victor in her feelings of anger and resentment. I was amazed at how quickly she forgave those who had made the obvious errors in judgment. She persevered getting the first doctor's appointment and coping with the ER doctor's lack of concern. That took courage and an act of the will-what agape love.

"I remember watching Kathy be a stabilizer and a comforter to her folks when she was also in pain and then acknowledging the healing of the Great Physician far greater than any earthly physician could possibly do."

A friend who quietly and faithfully came weekly to our home after Mark left the hospital wrote, "I learned simply being there and being myself was the best way to support and comfort."

These are a few of the testaments of love and care contained in an array of comments our friends gave us. We treasure these even though the "whys" still linger. Yet, how can we, who can't even know what will happen a moment from now, give a reason for suffering? We would play the fool, stepping into the role of Job's ignorant friends. What we have learned is that suffering is one means to greater love and generosity.

We continually thank God for bringing Mark back, if only to be an inspiration to the professor who complimented him for his dedication and diligence. "Keep up the progress," he wrote on one of Mark's papers. "God has a special ministry for you."

How grateful we are that Mark was one of the estimated 5% of brain injured patients who receive adequate care. He, indeed, has been chosen by God to help others.

18

Chosen

(by Mark)

o o o o o o o o o o o o o o o o o o o o o o o o o o o o o o o o o o o o o o

Strength is born in the deep silence of long-suffering hearts, not amid joy.

—*Felicia Hermans*

As I awake I often ask the same questions.

"Father, I'd have rather prepared for foreign missions. Why couldn't I have joined friends who felt this call?

Why couldn't I have been part of the norm? "Why have you chosen me to be unique?"

My balance is checked as I plod into the bathroom. My bare feet bend outward, and my ability to remain upright is threatened with each step.

"Things were different before the accident."

As I slip into clean clothes my balance is tested again. Lack of steadiness prevents me from standing to dress.

Preparing breakfast, cleaning the dishes, and other routine tasks take too long. I am frustrated by my inability to move quickly.

"Lord, why?"

While attending seminary and living at home, I resided with parents who had gone through the agony with me. But they actually experienced more. They painfully remembered when I lay as if lifeless. They lived through difficult days with consistent, comforting support.

"Help me learn from them, Father."

To this day, news coverage and conversations at work inform me of countless disasters. Riots. Diseases. Murders. Starvations. Governments in turmoil.

But I often feel distant and far removed from these events. I'm human, and to see the needs of others as greater than my own dilemmas challenges me. At times I have felt forgotten by God.

I always recognized His power, but portions of Scripture led me to question His benevolence. Isaiah 45:7 says, for example, "I form the light and create darkness, I bring prosperity and create disaster; I, the Lord, do all these things."

It seems impossible that <u>bara</u>, Isaiah's word that is translated "create," could align with the well-known creation story. The verb, however, is the same Hebrew root used in Genesis 1. That same word is translated "produced," "make," or "bring about" in other passages.

The "prosperity" Isaiah addressed (the Hebrew <u>shalom</u>) is translated "wellbeing" in the New American Standard Version. In other passages <u>shalom</u> is translated "completeness," "soundness," "welfare," or "peace." My heavenly Father provides wholeness and unity.

"Disaster" (the Hebrew <u>ra</u>), however, is found in the same sentence. The evil and distress described appear to conflict with peace. God brings well being, but He also authors calamity.

What I had interpreted as an insensitive uncaring Creator seemed to be asking me to worship him. Where had my loving, compassionate Father gone?

Another usage of <u>bara</u>, however, has to be considered. The same Hebrew root translated "create" in several passages is also used in Ezekiel 23:47.

In Ezekiel bara is translated "cut down."

Creation, I had assumed, honored and glorified God. Destruction did not align with this concept of Him.

Still, a comforting notion comes to mind: cutting something down will lead to increased growth and productivity.

God's nurturing consoles me. I see Him in His garden, pruning, watering, and cultivating. Tending seems destructive at times. Yet, God produces a refined product, a creation bringing greater recognition of Himself.

For a time, I had seen a God who delighted in creating disaster. But my training at WCBS provided fresh insight into God's methods. Our understanding of Scripture, for example, may be "wholly true," but it can never be "truly whole." As we read and process God's revelation, we mature in our knowledge of Him. In maturing, our concepts of God and His glory change. That change means growth.

Lamentations 3:32 repeats what is said in Isaiah, but includes another facet. "Though He brings grief," it reads, "He will show compassion, so great is His unfailing love."

God's tenderness continues to comfort me. I serve a Creator who hurts alongside me. When I cry, He weeps, too. When I suffer, He shares the pain. In His pruning process, my Father has cut me down, built me up again, and prepared me for a special ministry.

God is helping me accept my losses. In that ongoing process, He is equipping me to better understand the pains of others and contribute to their adjustments. With my counseling practicum at WCBS, God used me to encourage individuals to attain independence despite their disabilities. Often when clients spoke of their suffering, I had a sense of their hurts. I tried, also, to remind them that our griefs are balanced by God's compassion.

The counseling I provided others was God's design for me. It was not surprising that rehabilitation professionals and hospital personnel were thrilled when I invited them to my WCBS commencement. "I want to extend my heartiest congratulations and very best wishes," Dr. Ward stated. "We at RIO are proud of your accomplishments." "Our thoughts and prayers are with you," Carol Saxton and other Providence Hospital medical staff wrote.

"We are so happy for you," another supportive family wrote. "What you learned will stand you in good stead in future ministry—much perseverance and determination are needed. God will use you." Their card closed with, "Always believing in you."

A graduation reception hosted by the Zimmerman family brought a steady flow of family and friends. They had all supported me through my rehabilitation and training and shared my joy. A visit by Kathy and Steve from St. Paul highlighted the celebration.

God used my seminary experience to increase my confidence and assure me of His direction. His next step, however, required further refinement of my counseling skills through the Rehabilitation Counseling program at Portland State University. This schooling, internship, and eventual degree led to my certification and employment as a vocational rehabilitation counselor. I am enjoying opportunities to provide vocational rehabilitation services to individuals with disabilities that have interfered with employment and coordinate training or placement that will lead to their successful employment.

I have been honored, in addition, with promotion to a Vocational Rehabilitation Specialist position. I am privileged to gather additional information regarding traumatic brain injury and work adaptation services and share these resources with counselors throughout the state.

God has directed me throughout the Northwest as I have worked in Yakima WA, Klamath Falls OR, and again in my hometown, Portland OR. After securing state employment and purchasing a home, I felt His graciousness had been abundant and I could not ask for more.

My friendship with Linda Nakagawa, however, developed and blossomed. I was amazed at the interests and values we shared and the sheer enchantment I felt in her presence. On May 18, 2002 I married this beautiful woman who is composed, among other things, of spiritual maturity, charming humor, meaningful conversation, and endless delight. Linda is tremendous compensation for my limitations while accepting, respecting, and loving me as a complete individual. My time to dance has come!

May 18, 2002

I am grateful, but humbled, as I consider my journey. It had been assumed I would require 24-hour nursing care, but I attained two master's degrees and vocational counselor certification. I progressed from a patient with catastrophic insult to a vocational rehabilitation specialist focusing on traumatic brain injury.

Options proposed for me included residing in a care facility, but I lived independently for several years before purchasing a home and marrying. Instead of being subject to continual supervised care, sharing life with the helpmate He chose for me confirms His power, purpose, and love.

I praise God for Linda and the network of people He has given me to share in my comeback journey. My transition from victim to over-comer often seemed slow, arduous, and painful. I felt that moments of disappointment and despair accompanied what appeared to be a plodding, snail-pace journey. God's prescribed course many times has not been easy to understand, but sharing with others has lessened the pain.

Friends, medical and rehabilitation teams, and, most importantly, my family have supported me. My sister always encouraged me in my bleakest hours and prompted me to achieve in good times. My mother and father were, and still are, there for me, modeling their trust in God. Their consistent investment of time, care, and compassion are examples I strive to reflect in my counseling.[1]

I thank my Father for the continuing recovery He has authored. He, indeed, has a plan for my life. I pray that my journey will help others recognize that pruning leads to the growth and maturation He has designed.

---

1. Mark was recently appointed to the State of Oregon Traumatic Brain Injury Board.

EPILOGUE

WHEN GOING THROUGH A CRISIS

After, or even during, a crisis you need to take simple, practical steps toward healing. Begin by:

RECOVERING PHYSICALLY:

Eating three meals daily: Eat well-balanced meals to lessen your fatigue and moodiness. Poor diet may contribute to emotional imbalance. In spite of loss of appetite eat small amounts of healthy food regularly. Your appetite will gradually return.

Exercising regularly: Set up a daily exercise routine to boost your morale and lessen your stress. If you would like more structure, join a health club or simply take a brisk walk in the fresh air daily. Don't be discouraged with an initially low energy level. As you are consistent with a few minutes of daily exercise your capacity will increase.

Obtaining ample rest: Attempt to go to bed earlier, sleep in or take an occasional afternoon nap.

RECOVERING EMOTIONALLY:

Visualizing Happiness: Think about people who have helped make one of your prayers come true. The spontaneity of life can also be recaptured by: singing in the shower, taking the scenic route when returning home from an errand, watching a sunrise or sunset, relaxing on a lounge chair while gazing at the stars, taking pictures to capture precious moments, going to a movie, museum, zoo, or a park with a friend, sorting out old snapshots to enjoy pleasant memories, going beachcombing, for a nature walk, hike or jog, or inviting a friend over for a snack and good chat.

Learning to smile and laugh again: Give God a chance to mend your tattered soul by reading for recreation and re-creation. You needn't feel guilty if you laugh when reading a funny book, watching your favorite comedian on TV, or sharing jokes with a friend.

Getting in touch with your emotions: Reclaim a part of yourself by dealing with anger, guilt, despair, and fear. For some people, soaking in the tub with bubbles and lighted candles surrounded by their favorite music works. Give yourself permission to do nothing when you need space to catch your breath from repeated hospital visits or caring for your loved one at home.

Writing it down: Journal your daily thoughts to help release your emotions and to gain objectivity.

Talking it over: Share your feelings, fears, and memories with a friend you trust to hear you and to gain perspective on frightening "what ifs." Seek a friend who will patiently listen to your doubts and fears without condemnation. The most helpful friend will give loving, honest, positive feedback after listening. Talk to your pastor, a therapist, or small group for additional support.

Lightening up: As your budget and energy allows embark on a campaign inside your home. Light is therapeutic. Use off-white (except for the visually impaired) and pastel wall colors and keep the draperies or shutters open allowing in light. Fresh flowers, cheerful music, or a painting or two can lift your spirits.

Being creative: Retain happy memories but if some memories haunt you gradually replace them with new experiences. A meal out, a day off work, finishing a fun project, and a weekend away can help refresh and restore your mental and emotional balance.

Seeking Professional Help: Should your grief continue without end, sessions with a professional counselor can help resolve some of the guilt, anger, and despair that stands in the way of your recovery. Be assured that help for emotional healing is as essential as help for physical healing. Do not consider it a sign of spiritual or emotional weakness should short-term or long-term medication be required to re-establish your state of well-being. Because of a body chemistry imbalance, more than two percent of Americans require medication to lead a normal, healthy life.

RECOVERING SPIRITUALLY:

Staying in tune: Memorize and meditate on Bible verses and talk with God. These are vital parts of your recovery and spiritual journey. Write down (or discuss with a family member or close friend) what God is teaching you. Writing will clarify those deep lessons and will help you see practical ways to claim His strength one day at a time. A written record of your journey will bring encouragement as you periodically review all that God has done.

Offering prayers of petition and thanksgiving as you exercise daily.

As you create new memories and build new traditions, you lay a foundation for healing and a fresh outlook. Recovery is not a temporary "fix," it is a blueprint for the rest of your life. You will gradually arrive at a "new normal" that will please you.

Recovery is a piece of work you do, recycle, and redo. Part of that recovery is learning to take care of yourself. As you recover and discover you'll fully realize that your self worth rests in God's opinion of you. He regards you as priceless.

The author
hostess@hostesshouse.com
www.hostesshouse.com

CHAPTER 1

THOUGHT/ACTION PROVOKERS:

1. Jot down your reaction to the statement, "Grief is not a sign of weakness."

2. A support group under girds rather than confronts. Think through other pros and cons of the informal support group.

3. After having observed the value of our family-and-friend support group (pp. 4-6), which of the following should you do?

    •   Phone someone who is going through a crisis and let them know you care they are hurting.

    •   Provide a meal, send flowers or cards, or run errands for the family.

    •   Provide a tape recorder or radio for the patient so they can begin each morning with some favorite music. This helps set the tone for their day.

    •   Grasp a patient's hand or give a hug if it seems appropriate. Touch is important.

    •   Keep phone numbers of the family, the hospital, and the family's clergy near your telephone.

    •   Remind your prayer group to pray for your ill friend or family member.

    •   Be part of a support group at the hospital.

    •   Other possible actions?

4. In what ways have friends effectively helped you in times of crises? Evaluate why those actions were helpful. What actions have not been helpful? Why?

5. What circumstances can be worse than death? Why? Speak your heart.

CHAPTER 2

THOUGHT/ACTION PROVOKERS:

1. "The only way out is through." What does this statement mean?

2. J. William Worden, Ph.D., psychotherapist and researcher, says that the four tasks of successful mourning [for any major loss] are:

    •   to accept the reality of the loss.

    •   to experience the pain of grief.

    •   to adjust to the environment (in which there will be significant life changes).

    •   to withdraw emotional energy [in unrealistic hopes] and reinvest it in [a changed] relationship Grief Counseling and Grief Therapy, pp. 11-17, J. William Worden, Springer Publishing Company, Inc., 1982).

Does Warden's theory relate to a crisis of your own experience or that of others? In what ways?

    •   Using this theory as a reference, what correlation did you see in Mark's family crisis? Explain.

3. How can you express hope for the patient and family and at the same time be honest about their crisis?

4. Work through your own understanding of the first task of successful mourning-"to accept the reality of the loss"-so that you'll be prepared if the patient or members of the family ask for your counsel. Keep it simple.

5. What goals for the patient, family and friends do you hope will be obtained through their crisis? If you wish, make a list.

CHAPTER 3

THOUGHT/ACTION PROVOKERS:

1. How might the positive/negative interaction among our family and friends help you guide an individual going through a similar crisis? What other coping skills would you have used?

2. Contact a family member or friend who is hurting. Try one of the positive interactions described in this chapter.

3. Pain is inevitable in today's broken world. How can we deal with pain honestly rather than denying it?

4. A family member or friend feels "numb" at the onset of a crisis. How can you help them know that this is a normal reaction? A step toward accepting reality? (See Ch 2, #1&3)

5. Do you think the doctor's advice to the family, "Pace yourselves" (p. 20), was good counsel?

6. List some of the important responses that will help a patient cope with their crisis such as: (See Ch 1, #3)

   • speaking calmly and with respect;

   • voicing your love often; and

   • accepting abnormal behavior quietly.

7. Do you agree with the statement, "In times of grief we don't choose our emotions, they choose us? If you do, can you cite examples?

CHAPTER 4

THOUGHT/ACTION PROVOKERS:

1. A poster, "GOD IS THE BLESSED CONTROLLER OF ALL THINGS," was placed at the foot of Mark's bed (p. 23). "But my feelings didn't affirm this statement," says the author.

    • Think about this statement: What you know and what you feel during a crisis may conflict, and that's okay. What is your response?

2. What did Mark's parents decide would be their best personal coping therapy (p. 24)?

    • Do you think they made a wise choice?

3. Mark's doctor said Mark needed stimulation (p. 27). Do you believe that our talking to Mark when he was comatose stimulated him and aided his recovery?

4. What reaction do you have to posting in Mark's room a sign, "EVERYTHING SAID IN HERE MUST BE POSITIVE" (p. 30)?

5. How does a positive attitude help a patient?

6. Write down positive and negative actions you observed among the family and their friends in this chapter. How would you apply one or more of these positive actions to your family or friend's crisis?

CHAPTER 5

THOUGHT/ACTION PROVOKERS:

1.   What grief recovery tasks have you observed in this chapter?

   - Do you think the tasks can overlap? For example: the task of accepting reality and the task of grieving were being dealt with at the same time.

   - List some of the "pains of grief" experienced by the family.

2.   Individuals suffer losses as varied as divorce, health, death, job, abortion, bankruptcy, accident, miscarriage, violence, theft, suicide, expectations, and rape. Is the first step in healing each loss the acceptance of the reality?

3.   How have you been able to accept the reality of the loss experienced by a family member or friend? Or, what do you plan to do to assist a family member or friend who is going through a crisis?

4.   If a friend or loved one were dying, how would you deal with it? Does this chapter give you any ideas?

CHAPTER 6

THOUGHT/ACTION PROVOKERS:

1.   The author declares that she was angry at God (p. 37).

   - How do you reconcile spiritual "turmoil" with daily life? What happens when there is a conflict between the two?

   - Do you feel it is right or wrong to be angry at God or express anger toward God? Write your reasons for yourself or to share with another person.

   - Have you had a conflict in which your actions did not match your beliefs? Discuss this with a friend.

1.   What grief recovery task in this chapter impresses you?

2.   When Mark's college friends rallied around with prayers, visits, touches, and cards, do you think this gave deeper meaning to his life?

3.   Take your family member or friend something new to taste, play a tape or CD, share your vacation pictures, or take a pet for them to enjoy.

4.   For your benefit or to share in a group, write a paragraph describing how you have worked through feelings of fear, disappointment, or anger regarding the crisis of your family or friend.

5.   Write to your family member or friend in crisis expressing how you value their love and friendship and offer specific help.

CHAPTER 7

THOUGHT/ACTION PROVOKERS:

1. Is it ever right to make demands of God?

2. Do you believe there is a dimension beyond medical science that is outside a physician's control (p. 44)? If so, can you cite an example?

3. For a grief wound to heal, it must be kept clean and open. Write out what this statement means to you.

4. Have you ever been involved with a head trauma patient? If so, what areas of the "levels of awareness" list did you observe (pp. 44-45)?

5. Were Mark's parents wise in insisting that Kathy keep her three-year residency appointments (p. 47)?

6. Give your reaction to the nurse described on page (p. 48). What would you have done if you were Mark's mother?

7. What new insights did you learn in this chapter that might assist you in helping an ill friend or relative?

    *   Could you invite a grieving friend over for coffee?

    *   Are you a good listener?

    *   How about inviting this person out to lunch, dinner, or the theater?

    *   Could you create a positive memory for them along their recovery journey?

CHAPTER 8

THOUGHT/ACTION PROVOKERS:

1. "Love is not only something you feel, it's something you do." What examples of this statement can you identify in this chapter?

2. Should tragedy strike your family, who would provide support and encouragement?

3. If your family member or friend does not have a strong support group, what initial steps might they take to find such a group?

4. List some support groups who are helping your family member of friend survive their crisis.

5. "Hope is the honey which keeps the present sweet." How do you define hope?

6. Think about the statement, "Your mind entertains one thought at a time." How can you make your thoughts positive and constructive?

7. Through an act of kindness this week reach out to a family member or friend in crisis by visiting them, running an errand, or taking him/her to visit a friend or relative.

8. Recount some of the kindnesses others have extended to your ill family member or friend. Be specific.

CHAPTER 9

THOUGHT/ACTION PROVOKERS:

1. Think about Kathy's comments, "I hated God and thought of killing you, Mark, Dad, and myself" (p. 62). What are your reactions?

2. When the author slumped into a depression (p. 62), were you surprised?

3. What were some symptoms of a depressed person listed in the chapter (pp. 62 and 64)?

   - Can you understand the author's comment, "Seeing Mark this way hurts my heart and shakes my faith?"

   - Is it okay to have thoughts that contradict your beliefs?

4. Do you believe that denial of an emotional problem is healthy or dishonest?

5. Think about the statement, "If you are going to heal you have to feel." Believe it? Don't believe it?

6. Keep a daily journal and stay in touch with your feelings regarding the illness of your family member or friend. Write down your honest thoughts.

7. When the time and setting are appropriate to help a family member or friend recuperate from a serious accident or illness:

   - help them create something with their hands by experimenting with new mediums: clay, paint, finger paint, or pudding art (encourage them to lick their fingers);

   - place a bird feeder where the patient can see birds coming to feed. Encourage them to write down the names of the birds they can identify (check out a book about birds from your local library); or

   - talk to an occupational therapist about additional ideas.

CHAPTER 10

THOUGHT/ACTION PROVOKERS:

1. The author's older brother-in-law could not watch Mark struggle with his physical therapy (p. 75).

    • Can you accept the fact that individuals cope differently?

    • How do you cope when a beloved friend or relative lies helpless in the hospital?

2. How would you have handled the problem with the night nurse (p. 75)?

3. After a severe loss, the victim's ability to comprehend enough to know what words mean is a great step of progress.

    • Do you believe Mark has reached that level?

    • A friend asked Mark about his spiritual life and reprimanded him for not reading the Word. What is your opinion (p. 76)?

4. "Part of recovery is understanding that not everyone understands," statement from a seminar on grief release. What are your ideas?

5. What are your thoughts about Mark remembering Shirley Berglund (p. 77)?

6. What value do you see in Mark reading the Ezekiel chart (p. 78)?

7. Visit an ill relative or friend and reminisce about the past. Recall the incident that delighted the patient the most. Make a note for your next visit so you can enjoy it again.

8. Write a beloved relative or friend who has a chronic illness understanding they will come to depend on hearing from you.

9. Write to an ill friend or relative you care about and tell them why they are important to you.

CHAPTER 11

THOUGHT/ACTION PROVOKERS:

1. Who have you known who has been forced by illness or accident to give up their dignity? How did this make the person feel and react?

2. Why is the lack of sound judgment a common characteristic of a person coping with their crisis?

3. When a person like Mark experiences severe loss they often function in a fog and need help to make major decisions. How would you help an ill friend or relative in a similar situation?

4. How did Mark's accident give him motivation to move outside his own problems and counsel his friend who struggled with alcoholism (p. 86)? How did this help them bond?

5. How did moving outside his own problems and thinking about Cary's needs help Mark get rid of feeling like a victim (p. 86)?

6. Think about substituting the words, "Next time" for "if only" and "opportunity" for "problem" to heal the past and look forward to the future.

7. A person's greatest emotional need is to feel loved and appreciated. Give some examples.

8. Things you might do to help the person convalescing:

    •   Learn by gentle probing regarding his or her wishes and desires that you can fulfill. Make one of these wishes come true.

    •   Talk to the physical and/or occupational therapist and offer any help you can give to speed the patient's recovery. Find out about passive exercises-ask if playing number or letter games with the patient will help their recovery.

CHAPTER 12

THOUGHT/ACTION PROVOKERS:

1. "How could Anne have been so insensitive?" Bob asked. "It's hard for me to forgive her." Look at the circumstances from both of their perspectives. Give reasons for being supportive of either person (p. 92).

2. What would you have done if you were Anne?

3. The author was asked by David for approval to date Anne. She stated, "Privately I had released Anne, but I didn't yet feel the words I'd spoken" (p. 93). How would you explain this statement?

4. Suicidal thoughts flashed through Mark's mind during his deepest despair (p. 97).

    • Did this surprise you? Why or why not?

    • Why do you think that individuals who suffer severe losses often consider suicide?

5. For Mark, the Pastor's message was like listening to "fast-forward" on a cassette tape. Can you recount such a circumstance?

6. Visit a person who is experiencing deep guilt due to the loss of a friend or relative because of suicide. Listen to the person's concerns, letting them know you care they hurt. Or, reestablish a correspondence relationship with a critically ill friend of family member.

CHAPTER 13

THOUGHT/ACTION PROVOKERS:

1. "The person who is beaten understands the pain better than the person who observes the beating." How does this apply in Mark's family? Who do you think is suffering most? Why?

2. Because the stark reality of his life after the accident oppressed Mark, do you think he was being ungrateful dwelling on his losses (pp. 103-104)?

3. What is your reaction to the statement, "There is no timetable for grief recovery?"

4. What does Kathy's statement, "I can definitely say that I have seen God's supernatural power in bringing Mark back" (p. 107) say about her own struggle to believe?

5. How can you help your ill friend or family member resolve the gap between the person they now seem to be and the person you think you knew?

6. To get to know your convalescent friend or family member better, make it comfortable for them to share their feelings. Brighten their day. Say something honest that will encourage them.

7. Share memories and compare experiences with someone who is going through a loss. Be a good listener and be sensitive as to what and how much they want to hear from you.

8. Call an ill friend or relative and offer specific help. Let the person know how much time you can give.

CHAPTER 14

THOUGHT/ACTION PROVOKERS:

1. What is your reaction to the statement, "Grief is one of the most demanding jobs?"

2. How would you respond to the doctor's statement: "Mark, I've never before talked to anyone in an intelligent conversation who has been where you were" (p. 115)?

3. Do you agree that sometimes there are some things which may be better left unsaid (p. 115)?

   • When should the patient be given selective information?

   • When is it better not to overload the patient?

4. Suggest to your recovering friend or relative that they journal ways others have eased their grief recovery.

   • Offer assistance in writing a thank you to a friend for helping them through their crisis, then mail the note for them.

   • Have them focus on all the little steps that are helping them get well. Suggest writing them down and rereading them often.

5. Do something special for an ill person without telling then you were the giver-"random kindness and senseless acts of love."

CHAPTER 15

THOUGHT/ACTION PROVOKERS:

1. On page 124, Mark makes some perceptive comments about pain and patience. Reread this section and study the following before you visit someone with similar problems.

2. Some "do's" and "don'ts" for helping a person dealing with losses. Do:

    *   be aware of needs and offer to help in practical ways;

    *   practice empathy. Say, "I can't imagine how you must feel, but can you tell me about it?" Remember there are no magic words to take the pain away and there are no positive words to explain the situation;

    *   touch the person (but ask first);

    *   realize the person's sense of dignity and pride has been invaded;

    *   encourage expression of all feelings such as anger, grief, or confusion without dubbing the patient "good" or "bad";

    *   allow the "working through" of the loss. The victim of loss should be able to cry without feeling ashamed;

    *   avoid clichés such as, "This is God's will for you";

    *   trust God to show the person His will;

    *   support positive ways to express the loss;

    *   support the postponement of major decisions until the period of dealing with the loss has abated; and

    *   be patient. Individuals who experience losses take a long time to recover.

    Do not:

    *   assume you understand or have the answers;

    *   defend God;

- take advantage of the person's vulnerability;

- instruct or give advice-just help the person survive;

- do not attempt to tell the person how they feel;

- give your approval or disapproval;

- probe for details;

- try to find magic words to make the pain go away. There are none.

- try to find positive words to explain the situation. They don't work.

CHAPTER 16

THOUGHT/ACTION PROVOKERS:

1. A therapist has said, "Take baby steps toward healing recovery." What is your reaction to this statement?

2. Why do you think some individuals avoid or act differently toward a person after they have suffered a loss? Can you give examples of such behavior?

3. How do you relate to the statements, "I need to get out and see how much of me is really left" (p. 128) and "It hurts when you are separated from the norm" (p. 131)? How realistic and objective are Mark's comments?

4. "Forgiving someone doesn't make them right, but it sets you free". How did the author's battle with anger and resentment help her healing (p. 129)?

5. When Mark overextended himself his emotions collapsed (p. 129). Can you recall a similar situation? How did this person regain balance?

6. Do you think Mark was progressing when he said, "I want to be allowed to have some self-pity" (p. 133), or did he momentarily relapse?

    •   Is it okay to have self-pity?

    •   Do you agree with the statement that, "Acting out the pain is essential?"

7. The common denominator between a therapist and a support group is recovery. A therapist explores the problem. A support group under girds rather than confronts. Think through additional pros and cons of each (see Ch 1, #2)

8. Help someone to act out his/her pain by going for a walk, for a hike, or beach combing. Your job is to be a good listener.

CHAPTER 17

THOUGHT/ACTION PROVEKERS:

1. How do you respond to Mark's comment, "I feel like a half-miracle"? (p. 140).

2. The author states that her family's experience of being seasoned by suffering gave them increased credibility with others in crisis (p. 142). Do you find that when you share your hurts you build bridges? What happens when you share your successes? Cite examples.

3. To help yourself become a better helper practice forgiving yourself for a mistake you made. If this also offended another person, ask for forgiveness. If the person brushes it off by saying, "Oh, it was nothing, I've forgotten all about that," turn their apparent indifference into graciousness by replying, 'Thank you." Be sure you verbally forgive anyone who asks for your forgiveness.

4. Remember life isn't just about how to survive the storm but how to dance in the rain. Next time a crisis arises help the person "not waste their pain."

5. Smile. It's contagious. The exercise costs nothing and is beyond price.

CHAPTER 18

THOUGHT/ACTION PROVOKERS:

1. When confronted by a crisis, the true character of one's faith emerges.

    - How well is Mark adjusting to his losses? Where do you believe he is in his recovery journey?

    - How well is your friend or relative adjusting to loss? Where are they in their recovery?

2. How important are the attitudes of individuals regarding their losses? Who is affected by these attitudes?

3. Mark has come full circuit, from a TBI patient to a Vocation Rehabilitation Specialist focusing on traumatic brain injury. How will this experience help him be a more effective counselor?

4. Would you agree with the following statements?

    - It is okay to set high expectations.

    - Pain is part of life.

    - Problems can be opportunities for growth.

5. Do you believe that "a person who has had a loss must switch from victim/survivor (why me?) to an overcomer (what next?)?"

6. Think about the statement "loneliness is the ultimate poverty."

7. Shakespeare said, "I am wealthy in my friends."

    - How does this apply to Mark's circumstances?

    - How does this apply to your relative or friend's circumstances?

8. For most people, especially those working through losses, life is a daily process. What goal have you set for helping your hurting relative or friend recover? Remember, too, time does not heal. Recovery heals and recovery takes time and there is no time-line for recovery.

CPSIA information can be obtained at www.ICGtesting.com
Printed in the USA
BVOW02s2048091013

333344BV00001B/4/P